## SHANE BAUTISTA

Shane was born on the 21$^{st}$ of June 1978. At the age of Five, he began Ice figure skating before having to stop after the Dandenong Ice skating rink closed. At the age of fifteen, Shane worked professionally as an actor, singer, and dancer. Shane joined The Johnny Young Talent School in Richmond and won his first lead role in an education video starring alongside Collette Mann *(Prisoner & Neighbours)*.

When he turned eighteen years old, he joined an adult acting agency 'Linda's Rising Stars' and worked on numerous TV Series as (an extra and bit parts) including 'Neighbours' (Channel Ten), 'Good Guys Bad Guys' (Channel Nine) 'Raw FM' (ABC), Feature Film 'River Street' filmed in Melbourne and danced in a Japanese TV Commercial for Sony, filmed in Melbourne.

In the year 1999, Shane completed a Bachelor of Arts Degree at Deakin University where he completed a double major in Graphic Design/Photography and Visual Arts and minored in Public Relations & Contemporary Dance. He then began working for Fairfax local newspaper 'The Dandenong Leader as a Graphic Designer. While working full-time, Shane won a lead role in a semi-professional ChristianTheatre Company playing the role of 'Jalam' in on original musical production titled 'Winter Thaw' based on 'The Lion, Witch, and the Wardrobe. For the next two years, he travelled with the Theatre Company around Melbourne and toured Sydney during the 2000 Olympic Games.

In 2002 Shane left Graphic design and started training at the Jannz School of Singing with David Jaanz, teaming up with newcomer music producer, *Sarah Godden* and recorded his EP which included hits 'Play Me' which can be found on his artist's page under 'Triple J Unearthed'. Shane performed live at Melbourne's LGBTIQ Midsummer Festival in 2003 and 2004 and at the Midsummer pool party in Melbourne's suburb Fitzroy where he was interviewed by Gretel Killeen who hosted 'Let's Talk About Sex' (Channel Ten).

In 2004 Shane moved to Sydney to pursue his acting, dancing and singing career and danced in the 2005 Sydney Gay and Lesbian Mardi Gras final after-party show at Fox Studios. After only six months in Sydney, Shane returned to Melbourne and trained full time at The Dance Factory in Richmond.

Shane left the entertainment industry at age twenty-eight and pursued a career in the corporate world for three years. In 2010 Shane worked as a Personal Trainer while completing his 2$^{nd}$ Bachelor's Degree in Health Science - *Myotherapy*. During 2011, Shane recommenced skating at the Olympic Ice-Skating Rink in Melbourne's Docklands skating in the adult synchronised team and performing at the 2011 Christmas Concert. Upon completion, in 2012 he opened his own business for the next five years subcontracting out of various gyms in Melbourne. Unfortunately, during training in 2012, Shane had an accident and dislocated his right ankle and fractured his tibia, which ended his skating.

The year 2015, Shane returned to further study undertaking a Bachelor of Nursing. Upon completion, he started a graduate year in one of Victoria's most extensive public health services as a Registered Graduate Mental Health Nurse in 2018. During his graduate year, he presented at the Melbourne University Collaborative Conference on promoting physical health with people with Severe Mental Illness. He then went onto present a poster presentation at the Australian College of Mental Health Nursing (ACMHN) International Conference in Cairns, Australia. Shane was the only graduate to have presented at two conferences and be published in the ACMHN Summer news Magazine.

Resilience: a story of survival is Shane's memoir as an up and coming author. Shane is a entrepreneur running two business as a Myotherapist and making essential oil blends & candles with his sister Christine. He continues working as a Mental Health Nurse and hopes his memoir can help a lot of people find hope and resilience.

Shane currently resides in Melbourne, Victoria in Australia.

# RESILIENCE

## A SURVIVAL STORY

2019

BAUTISTA PUBLISHING

Book design by Green Hill Self-Publishing Australia 2019

Published by Bautista Publishing 2019

www.bautistapublishing.com

www.shanebautista.com



National Library of Australia
Cataloguing in Publication entry

Bautista, Shane, author

Resilience: a memoir

ISBN 978 0 6485862 6 5

1.Bautista, Shane. 2. Ward of the State – Australia - Foster care. 3.Substance
Abuse – Australia - Gay Men. 4.Mental Health – Suicide - Australia.

Cover Photography by Paul Burnett
paullaurance.com

Cover Design by Green Hill Publishing - Australia
Interior design by Green Hill Publishing -Australia
Typeset in 10/15 pt Minion Pro by Green Hill Publishing - Australia

Book was edited by Belinda Raposo

Cover Photography by Paul Burnett

This memoir is dedicated to the following people
in my life who have now passed.


**Brendan Andrew Prosser**

18/03/1982 – 07/03/2018

*My first real love, who loved me unconditionally but found his demons
too hard to live with anymore 'I Love you to the moon and back.'*


**Carmel Johnson**

1958 – 2018

*You were like a mother to me. You lost your fight with Cancer but
ended up in peace instead, I've done what you asked of me the last
time I saw you. I watched out for your son, my best mate, he is
doing well. You would be proud of what he has achieved.*


**Brian Leslie Graham**

11/07/1941 – 18/02/2002

*You gave me everything that my biological father could not,
and I'll never forget you and I'll always call you Dad*


**Betty Wakefield   &   Charlie Wakefield**

26/03/1918 – 1983          29/04/1919 – 1989

*My Grandparents – You brought me up for the first five years
of my life, Nan I wish you lived longer & pop was my mate,
thank you for being such wonderful grandparents.*

**WARNING**

This story discusses foster care & state government care, sexual abuse, grief, mental health issues, suicide, domestic violence, sexuality, substance abuse, addiction, and same-sex attraction and sexual themes. This book is best suited towards mature audiences of 16 + years. If you or someone you know is affected by any issues discussed, please seek help.

### Call Lifeline any time on 13 11 14

**DISCLAIMER**

People mentioned in this book have been given pseudonym names to protect particular individuals privacy and are purely fictional. Any resemblance of names to persons living or deceased is purely coincidental. My foster family and some of my biological family have given permission to use their first names only.

# CONTENTS

# PROLOGUE

Sometimes I wonder why I was born. What is my purpose in life? Why didn't I have a healthy family upbringing like other kids? Why wasn't I born straight? Why do I have a mental illness, and why did I have to struggle so much throughout my life? I could do my head in asking these questions, and yes there were times I wished I was someone else, had a different experience or even that I was dead.

Throughout my younger years, I struggled to fit in, and for a long time, I felt broken and dead inside. I quickly learned how to create a facade that resembled a confident, happy-go-lucky, carefree guy on the outside; when the truth was, I loathed myself, found it hard to care for and love myself because in my head were the inner voices telling me I was worthless, ugly and a waste of space. The inner demons always reminded me that my parents didn't want me, my extended family didn't want me; I was an unwanted child. No one would ever love me.

From an early age, I lived a life of trauma. However, I was a lucky kid that found myself in a loving foster family that I was able to stay with until I aged out of the foster care system at eighteen years old. There are a lot of adverse outcomes for kids that have come out of the foster care system. They either end up homeless, living a life of crime and ending up incarcerated, abusing drugs and alcohol or becoming teenage parents and repeating the cycle that they were born into, having their own children removed and placed in foster care.

For me, I wanted to change my outcome in life. I felt like I always struggled, that even when I was getting somewhere, kicking goals and achieving there was still something that would make me stumble and fall. *But life wasn't meant to be easy.* I had to work hard to change my life's story from victim to victor.

For a long time, I battled with shame, stigma and grief and loss. I was an unwanted child, molested at the age of six years old, and a gay male that used drugs for fun and to escape my inner demons and my life. I had sex with a lot of guys that showed me attention because I so desperately wanted to feel a connection. Giving my body to the men I liked led me to believe that they might fall in love with me.

I live with mental illness - attachment disorder as a child, personality disorder traits, depression, anxiety, self-harm, and suicidal behaviours. With all these labels I somehow, even in my darkest moments, could still find the strength within to pick myself up and keep moving on with my life, also when my thoughts are telling me to end it all. I take a high dose of anti-depressant medication, and just like someone on high blood pressure medications, my antidepressant keeps me well, like a well-oiled machine.

At the ripe age of forty, I finally found my purpose in life. As a Registered Mental Health Nurse, I hope to use my story to help others. For the youth currently in foster care or struggling with their sexuality and identity, I hope that reading my story can give them hope and encouragement to see that there can be a light at the end of the dark and lonely tunnel.

Writing my memoir, I wanted to stay true to myself and not worry about what content or themes would offend some people. A lot of my life is dark, but I have been lucky enough to have people in my life that have shone light through my darkness. Through experiencing early childhood trauma, I became a boy that had no sense of belonging either culturally, with self or feeling a connectedness to the life I was living. I hated myself so much that I self-harmed, had ongoing suicidal thoughts and an unsuccessful suicide attempt.

Throughout my story, there are 'gay' sexual themes in which I wanted to keep my sexual experiences tastefully descriptive, raw and confronting. Talking about sex for some people is uncomfortable, but for me, I find it liberating and at times funny. For the uneducated in the world of 'the gays', I have provided some inside knowledge that may shock you, intrigue you or answer questions that you have always wanted to know.

Throughout my memoir I will take you on a journey of how I survived my life thus far, and even when there were times I thought I couldn't go on anymore, I always found this innate resilience deep inside that I could use to bounce back and keep on going with life and never give up. I hope that my story can help others who are struggling with a similar background to mine and that it gives them hope to keep moving forward and create their own success story.

# CHAPTER 1

# REGRET

Sitting in the waiting room for my doctor's appointment, my mind was racing. I couldn't believe my stupid error of judgment. *What was I thinking?* I was so angry with myself. I started to feel my chest becoming tight, my heart beating faster. Finding it hard to breathe the palms of my hands began to get clammy – *what if I'm positive?* I tried calming myself down by doing some deep breathing techniques a counsellor in the past had taught me. *Breathe in through your nose slowly for two counts and breathe out through your mouth for four counts.* I could feel my heart slowing down, my breathing becoming more comfortable.

I peered around the clinic while doing my breathing exercises. The walls were adorned with posters about safe sex and protecting yourself against HIV and STI's. Seeing this wasn't helping, so I focused my attention on the guys waiting in the waiting room. A nice distraction. Sitting opposite me was a good-looking guy in his thirties, masculine build, messy, short brown hair and wearing a tight black singlet, blue jeans and thongs. He had a nose piercing and a half sleeve tattoo on his right arm. I couldn't quite make out what the symbol was, but it was black with different patterns that were distorted by his muscular biceps.

He busted me looking and, embarrassed, I smiled and quickly looked down. I snuck a quick glance again, but he was now occupied with a magazine he was reading. I felt like my mild panic attack had ceased thanks to the sexy muscle guy sitting across from me. But then again, sex was the last thing on my mind. In fact, I couldn't think of anything worse right now. It was casual sex that had put me in this situation. Jeff and Dylan had both assured me they were clean, but how can you be sure? *God, how did I end up here?*

I wanted to point the finger at someone else, so I blamed Ricco. I had fallen in love hard with Ricco, and I thought our relationship was going somewhere, but at the three-month mark, it was over. Ricco told me that he wasn't in love with me. I was crushed. So, on a Friday night that week, I went down my old, familiar self-destructive path, getting high, drunk and having sex with the first guy who wanted me.

I had met Ricco three months earlier at the largest gay club in Prahran, 'The Market'. The Market was the place to go and party on a Saturday night. My friends and I would start with pre-drinks at someone's apartment and then walk down to the club around 11pm. We were all club members, so we got free entry and access to the VIP line and didn't have to wait in long queues. Being able to walk straight in gave us that feeling of exclusivity, sense of importance, especially when you walked past the long line of people that were either new to the club or only came out occasionally. They didn't see the value in buying a membership like we did.

I wasn't always confident in approaching new people, but once we dropped ecstasy and it started to kick in, all my inhibitions disappeared. I felt invincible, confident and sure of myself. There was no room for my usual negative self-doubt as the influx of the feel-good hormones of serotonin and dopamine flooded my brain. Most Saturday nights were a bit of a blur. I loved the euphoric feeling the drugs gave me. I could escape my past and myself for the night. For that night, I could be whoever I wanted to be, and nobody really knew me. I could be someone else, the party boy, a reinvention of myself, a gay Madonna.

My friend Brent, who I had met a year ago while working at a post office in Melbourne - was my first gay friend. Brent had been on the gay scene a lot longer than me and knew a lot of people but being a 'young gay' as he liked to call it, would introduce me to guys when we were out. This night, it was while Brent was chatting away to a guy and girl sitting on a bench seat, that I saw him. *He is gorgeous! Look at his muscles!* There was a space where I might be able to sit next to him and start up a conversation, so I plonked myself down next to him.

"Hey, how's your night?" I asked.

"Yeah, good. I'm Ricco" he replied.

"I'm Shane, you're really hot by the way" I said confidently.

Ricco laughed, saying "Thanks, you're not too bad yourself."

Ricco was a cute Italian guy a couple of years younger than me. He looked like he worked out, with a stocky build and a great smile that drew me in straight away.

"You look like you're flying!" I observed.

"Yeah, I think my pill has kicked in" Ricco said.

"Yeah me too" I replied. Then I leaned in and kissed Ricco.

Kissing on ecstasy, or 'e' as we called it, felt amazing. Every sense in my body was alert, and it felt like it was the best kiss I had ever had. So passionate, sensual. You can't get enough.

Ricco and I moved to the dance floor downstairs. Dancing and kissing; mostly kissing. As the drugs became stronger, it was hard to see more than two feet in front of me. Ricco grabbed my hand and walked me back up the stairs until we got to the bean bags in a dark corner of the room. Laying on top of him, we then made out for what seemed most of the night. Things started to get hot and heavy, and I usually would be self-conscious, but the drugs running through my brain killed any of my inhibitions. *I didn't give a shit!* Ricco pushed me up onto my knees, and before I knew it, he was doing things to me, you shouldn't do in a club. As I looked around to see if anyone had noticed, I could see the guys sitting around were none the wiser, or maybe this was nothing new. The drugs heightened the sensation, and my orgasm was so intense I collapsed next to him, trying to inconspicuously put it back in my pants.

"Wow, I wasn't expecting that!" I said.

Ricco smiled cheekily, "I couldn't wait".

For the next three months, I had a boyfriend. I felt fulfilled, in love, and wanted. We saw each other nearly every other day, and instead of going out clubbing on the weekend we would stay home watching movies, cuddle on the couch, have mind-blowing sex– repeat. When we first started dating, we both got tested for STI's and HIV, and with both being negative, we started having unprotected (raw – the gay term) sex. Going raw felt better than a condom, and I felt closer, more intimate – *connected*. Ricco was a 'top' (the giver), and I became the 'bottom' (the receiver). One Sunday afternoon, my housemate was out for the day and Ricco, and I spent the afternoon making love. Each time we made love, I felt closer to him with every moment.

Being new to this, I had only bottomed a few times with my first ever boyfriend when I came out a year before. I enjoyed that position better anyway as the male G-spot is the prostate gland. He would kiss me tenderly, slowly kissing down my back. Holding me close with his muscly arms made me feel loved and protected. Lying next to him being held in his arms, I thought I had found the man of my dreams, I was undeniably in love.

The following week we had reached the three-month mark of us being together. The three-month mark in any relationship being same-sex or heterosexual seemed to signal the crossroad of a decision to make, whether you move ahead or turn left or right and leave it all behind. In my head, I definitely thought we would move forward and spend the rest of our lives together. I couldn't have been more wrong. Ricco decided to turn right and leave me behind. One night we were lying in bed after making love when he turned to me with a troubled look on his face.

"How much do you like me?" he asked

"I'm falling in love with you" I confidently said. He paused and looked up towards the ceiling and took a breath. I could feel it in the pit of my stomach, I knew what he was going to say before he could find the words.

"Please don't hate me, I'm not feeling it" he said.

"What?" I asked, but I already knew the answer.

"I knew pretty quickly, and I know the feeling hasn't happened for me like it has for you, and I really wish it had because I think you're amazing, I'm not in love with you I'm sorry" he said with tears in his eyes.

I was shocked and devastated when he said he wasn't in love with me. He said he was attracted to me but not in love. I was rejected. I felt like a child again, hearing that my mother didn't love or want me. My stomach turned in knots, and I felt my throat tighten. I tried to be brave and fight the tears, but I was overcome with emotional pain, rejection and disappointment. I cried in his arms as he held me tight. I was confused.

If he didn't love me, why did he act like he did? He kissed me so tenderly as the tears rolled down my face. I asked him if he needed more time. Pleading with him that maybe we just needed more time together, but he said no, he already knew, and nothing would change. Then suddenly, I stopped crying mid-sob and turned from a blubbering mess to someone cold, like my emotions had just suddenly disappeared. I pushed him away and started to lose my shit.

"Well you better go then" I coldly ordered him.

"Please don't be like this, we can talk" he pleaded.

"Talk about what Ricco? You don't love me! So, what the fuck are you doing here?" I shouted.

"We could still be friends?" he asked.

"Friends" I scoffed. We sat there in silence until I couldn't stand having him in my room anymore.

"I think you should go" I said.

Ricco got dressed and leaned in to kiss me goodbye, but I turned away.

"Ok, well, I guess I'll see you around" Ricco said.

I didn't answer him, and when I looked up, he was gone. I was devastated. I cried myself to sleep that night and ended up staying in bed all weekend. Heartbroken and alone, I kept checking my phone for any messages from him, but there were none. It took every ounce of my will to stop myself from contacting him. I wanted to hear his voice so badly, feel his skin, his tender kisses. These thoughts started to become so obsessive that I started to feel crazy. And like someone heartbroken, I tried to distract myself with chocolate, and romantic comedy chick flicks. 'Sex and the City' was my go-to, the Manhattan girls always cheered me up.

As the weeks passed, I grew from depressed to angry. It was a Friday night, and I found a bag of Ketamine left over from last weekend. Ketamine (we called it Special K or K) is generally used as a horse tranquilliser or for medical purposes for people that are allergic to other anaesthetics. In small doses, K gives you the feeling of being drunk but without the hangover the next day. It's typically snorted through the nostrils and leaves an acidic taste when it drips down the back of your throat, so flavoured drinks help. One night at the Market I had a pill that had a lot of K in it, and I ended up in a 'K hole' which meant I had too much and ended up half tranquilised for two hours, paralysed, sitting and looking over the dance floor on the second level of the club. K gave you a feeling of an out-of-body experience with separation from mind and body. Dancing and sex were terrific on it. Kissing a hot guy on the dance floor, you feel electric, every sense soaring through your body. After my K hole experience, I only did small bumps off my house key or short lines, snorting it up my nose using whatever dollar note I had in my wallet.

High and drunk on vodka and raspberry lemonade I had mixed into an empty soft drink bottle, I ended up at the gay sauna in Prahran. A sauna is a sex on site premises where guys can have the freedom to have no-strings-attached sex with strangers. Anonymous sex was what I thought I needed to make me feel wanted, even if by a stranger. I felt if Ricco didn't want me, then I would find someone that did. The sauna was down a dark one-way street that ran along the train line.

The outside looked like an old factory with coloured brown bricks that went up two stories, with a red light outside the entrance door. No signs, very discreet. I had never been to a place like this before, and I was feeling a little nervous, self-conscious. There was a man in his late forties behind the desk wearing a blue t-shirt and light blue, denim jeans. He had a slim build, and a septum ring like you would see on a bull so the farmer could lead him around. He had tatts that covered both his forearms. He looked rough, but he was sweet, calming and friendly. His smiled eased my anxiety.

"Fifteen dollars thanks" he smiled.

I nervously gave him the money while thinking *should I back out and go home?* It was like he could read my mind or just observed my awkwardness.

"First time?" he asked.

"Yeah" I awkwardly answered.

"Don't be nervous, there are a few hotties here tonight."

He handed me a red towel and a locker key with the number five written on it. He pointed to the red door beside me and smiled.

"Have fun' he said."

"Thanks."

As I opened the door, I was faced with a corridor full of lockers. I searched for number five, and as I turned the corner, I noticed a naked man standing at an opened locker. He looked like he was in his thirties, his body was toned with trimmed chest hair, a six pack and his butt cheeks had little dimples. I couldn't help but stare at his perfect body. I started to feel myself get hard as I watched him dry his wet body. He looked European and was well endowed. He noticed me staring. He looked back at me with his brown eyes and gave me a cheeky smile. I had just been sprung, so I quickly turned away, and as I turned my head, I hit it on the lockers beside me. *Fuck how embarrassing!* Smiling to himself while he put on his blue jocks, he asked "Are you OK?"

"Yep, just a little trashed" I replied, laughing.

"You been here, long?" I asked him.

"Couple of hours and now I'm going home. After seeing you, I now wish I could stay."

I was shocked by his compliment, but it felt good to be attractive to someone else.

"Why don't you?" I asked.

"I have work early tomorrow morning, I might see you here again sometime" he said.

"Maybe" I replied. The sexy Italian stallion had finished dressing, and as he walked past me, he ran his hand along the top of my bum, saying 'nice arse'. *Just stay for another hour,* I thought as I watched him leave the locker room.

I found my locker and started to undress, wrapping the towel around my waist, and then placing the elastic band that the key was tied to around my wrist. As I made my way through the darkness, waiting for my eyes to adjust to the red lighting, I soon found myself in a maze of black walls with mirrors at the end of each corner turn. There were little rooms you could take someone into. Inside each room was a bench bed with a thin mattress covered in vinyl, a box screwed to the wall full of condoms and next to it a pump that you see in the public toilets for soap, but instead of soap the pump boxes were full of lube.

Guys would stand near each door, waiting for someone to follow them inside the room. The smell of condoms and lube filled the air while the odd groans of pleasure could be heard from the private rooms. There wasn't much talent around, so I walked up the stairs hoping that there were guys more my type gathered there. The K had slowed everything down, and it felt like it took forever to walk up the stairs. It was when I reached the top that I saw Jeff. Jeff was a resident DJ at the X Change hotel, a pub/club down the road from the Market. It's where you would go for pre-drinks and watch the drag shows before heading to the Market on a Saturday night. Jeff was twenty-eight and had brown short messy hair, was straight acting and not at all the typical gay stereotype of a real feminine guy I had seen on TV shows. He was more my type.

I used to talk to him after he played his set and I had a major crush on him, but never thought he would go for someone like me. Then one night I thought I'd won the lottery. We had gotten drunk, and he kissed me, and I ended up going home with him. I wanted to date him, but he wasn't the commitment type, so we just stayed friends. When I was with Ricco, I didn't see him for three months as my focus shifted and it was all about Ricco. At the sauna, Jeff spotted me as I walked around the corner.

"Hey Mr" he said.

"Hey yourself" I replied coyly.

"You looked trashed! What have you had?" Jeff laughed.

"K" I replied.

"Got any more?" Jeff asked.

We walked back down to my locker. I pulled out the bag of K from my jeans pocket and gave him a bump.

"Thanks" he smiled as he leaned in and kissed me. I remembered how good a kisser he was. Jeff then grabbed my hand. "Follow me" he said as he led me back up the stairs and into one of the rooms. Inside waiting was a guy with spiky black hair. His chest was muscular, followed by a six pack and a black tattoo sleeve of a lion in the jungle down his right arm.

"Shane this is Dylan" Jeff said, introducing us. I replied with a coy "Hi".

Jeff kissed me as Dylan started kissing my neck. My body felt on fire; I was anxious, nervous, excited all at the same time. It felt good having two guys paying me this kind of attention, and it didn't take long before I became more confident. Eventually, I was on my back while Jeff positioned himself over me, and Dylan began kissing down his back.

"Can I fuck you?" Jeff asked.

"Yes," I nodded.

Jeff handed me a small bottle of amyl and I held it to both nostrils and inhaled. Amyl, or Amyl Nitrate, is also known as poppers, ram, thrust, rock hard, kix and TNT. When sniffed, amyl gives you a short-lasting head rush, like cocaine, and a feeling of your head being squeezed from all directions. I had heard that it enhances the orgasm and relaxes your anal muscles, which makes anal sex more enjoyable. Jeff felt so good. I had never been involved in a threesome before; it was fun, new and exciting and a great distraction. Dylan did Jeff while Jeff did me. Time was lost, and it seemed like hours had passed, then Jeff said he might go and try and find a fourth guy to join us.

While Jeff was out of the room, Dylan and I sniffed another dose of amyl. He pulled me on top of him. The rush of the amyl turns you into a sexual animal. He slid me onto him as we kissed passionately and then said "Stand up and bend over here" pointing to the mattress bed. Dylan was robust and a good lover. I felt weak and hazy as the amyl began to do its job. I felt like I was floating like I wasn't standing anymore, and my feet had left the ground. I loved this feeling, the feeling of pure ecstasy.

Then suddenly I came crashing back to earth as I felt Dylan fucking me harder and faster. Dylan held me so tight I could feel his heartbeat pounding on my back. I pretended for a moment it was Ricco, I missed him so much. Then suddenly I felt Dylan's hips press hard against my arse, holding that pose for about a minute before collapsing against my back exhausted. That's when I realised he had come inside me - *but I didn't care.* I was so desperate for some sort of connection. Even from the hot guy I knew nothing about other than he was great sex! Jeff walked back into the room, saying, "No one was up for it, so it's just us." Dylan, dripping with sweat, told us he was done and was going to have a rest. He kissed us both then left.

"Well I want to finish", Jeff said.

"Me too", I smiled.

Jeff lay me back on my back, and when Jeff kissed me, it was like he was making love to me. Jeff felt amazing and knew what he was doing.

"I want us to finish together" he said.

And we did. With K in my system and another sniff of amyl, we came at the same time, making our sexual encounter feel so intense. Jeff lay next to me, sweaty and exhausted. It was the first time since Ricco that I had felt that close to someone. But I couldn't fool myself into thinking that it was anything more than just a fuck. It wasn't like Jeff would suddenly get over his commitment issues and declare his love for me. As we lay there cuddling Jeff turned to me and kissed me.

"Thanks mister, I had a good time, did you?" he asked.

Looking into his brown eyes, I smiled, "Yeah I did, you're amazing".

He just laughed that comment off, saying "You're too kind". We lay there kissing and talking, stroking each other's backs. I wished this feeling of being loved could last forever, but I knew better than to think so unrealistically. My first threesome was incredible, but once I sobered up, all I felt was regret.
"Shane Bautista?"

Doctor Chung was an Asian-Australian man in his late twenties and was to do the tests which would decide my fate.

"Yes", I answered.

I walked over to him, and he ushered me into his treatment room. He asked me how he could help. I asked for an HIV test and explained my situation. He reassured me that often HIV positive guys self-disclose their status, but there is always a risk when drugs and alcohol are involved. He took some blood and gave me a plastic cup and long cotton-tipped stick. I had to provide a urine sample by pissing in the container and have an anal swap by putting the cotton tip up my arse.

"When you're done, pop the cotton sticks back in the plastic tube and put the lid back on the urine cup and place them in this plastic bag" he instructed.

As I returned to his room from the toilets, I handed the bag back to him.

"The test takes about a week" he informed me.

"OK". I said.

It had been three months since my encounter with Jeff and Dylan. On Saturday the morning after the threesome with Jeff and Dylan, I had gone to Dr Chung for a Post Exposure Prophylaxis (PEP) which is a four-week course of two pills you can take when you think there could be a possibility of being exposed to HIV. I had already waited for three months. What was another week? As I walked out of the clinic, all I felt was shame and anxiety in the pit of my stomach. I wondered how I had gotten here. *What have I done? How could I be so stupid? I mean the sex was great. Mind-blowing. But not worth this. How the fuck did I get here?*

The week waiting for my HIV/STI results felt like an eternity. I found it hard to sleep, lying there awake for hours just thinking about what I would do if I tested positive. I kept telling myself I would be fine, but the fear would creep its way through to taunt me. I didn't have anyone to confide in, I was too embarrassed to tell anybody. The one person I wanted to get me through this was Ricco, but I couldn't bring myself to call him to let him know what I had done. When I did finally tell Ricco what I had done, he was angry. I kept telling him how much I loved him, hoping that he magically felt the same way, but he didn't. Ricco was so disgusted in me that he stopped speaking to me. I felt so alone.

What if I was positive? I would have given myself a death sentence. All these ruminating thoughts seem ridiculous now with the advances of HIV treatment, enabling HIV posi-tive people living long and fulfilling lives. If an HIV positive person's viral load is undetectable, this means that there is zero chance of this person infecting someone that is HIV negative. However, I kept thinking about all the people in my life and how they would react to the news. I knew it would upset them and I didn't want to do that to anybody, nor did I want to be judged either. There is still a stigma around HIV and a fear of getting infected by other gay guys that don't quite understand the advances in HIV medicine today.

As the time came for me to find out my results, I found myself sitting in the waiting room at Prahran Medical Clinic in silence. My heart was pounding, I was scared, terrified. I waited for half an hour and finally, Dr Michael Chung came out holding my file. As he looked at me, I tried to read his facial expression, but he didn't give anything away, he had a good poker face. I guess he has dealt with a lot of HIV tests and broken the bad news, it was his job to remain neutral.

"Shane Bautista?" He called out.

"Yes," I replied.

"Come this way" he said, smiling as he ushered me with his hand towards his treatment room. As I followed him into his treatment room, I wished that I had superpowers like x-Rey vision to see what the results were in the file he was carrying. It turns out that all the blood test results are stored in a system on his computer, so there goes that idea!

I sat down on a chair next to his desk. I could feel the palms of my hands become sweaty. My throat tightening as he begins reading out the results.

*"OK, the results have a negative result for any STI's, so that is great! And the HIV test has come back negative as well, so you're in the clear!"* Dr Chung said.

I was so overwhelmed with the emotions I had been bottling up for the last three months. I didn't say anything to my friends out of shame, and I didn't really have anyone that I could talk to that would have understood without projecting their fear or judgement. Dr Chung handed me some tissues. I felt embarrassed that I was crying, but he was kind and comforting.

Dr Chung started giving me the lecture around safe sex.

*"You've been lucky this time. When you are on drugs, you feel invincible and your judgment is impaired. Next time you might not be so lucky, so make sure you play safe and make the other guy put on a condom"* Dr Chung kindly ordered.

I thanked him, he smiled and shook my hand to say goodbye. As I left the clinic I felt a new lease on life, a second chance. I thought about what he said and I always got tested every three months without fail. I had and promised myself never to put myself in that situation again. Who was I kidding? This was only the beginning of my reckless and risky behaviour.

# CHAPTER 2

# CHILDHOOD TRAUMA

As a two-year-old, the safest place for me was the darkness underneath my bed. My mother's epileptic seizures were the scariest things to watch as a toddler. Underneath my bed was the safest, I felt when things would go wrong. I used to hide out on two occasions, when my mother had her epileptic seizures and when she would be pissed off at my father. When my mother could feel a seizure coming on, she would lie on the couch. I would watch in horror as her jaw would clench tight. Her entire body would stiffen and thrash around, saliva would drool out of her mouth and sometimes her face would turn blue as her seizure took hold.

The seizures would last for thirty seconds then would suddenly stop. Mum would gasp for air and try and sit up, disorganised and confused as to what just happened, trying to breathe. This was the scariest part for me. The first time I saw mum having a seizure, I thought that she was dying. We were alone in the house and there was no one to help her. Afterwards mum would sleep for a few hours and when she awoke, would have no recollection of the seizure even taking place.

Another time mum had a seizure was when she was taking me to the toilet. I cried in fear, calling out "Mummy! Mummy!" The toilet door was open, but when she fell back, she had grabbed the door and it shut behind her as she hit her back and head, crashing against it. When the seizure stopped, I tried to wake up my mum, but she went into her deep sleep, and we were stuck in the toilet for an hour before she woke up. This time she knew she'd had a seizure. As she pulled herself up from the floor, she knelt on her knees and hugged me.

"Mummy's sorry for scaring you, darling."

This was the only time I can remember mum showing me love and affection before she disappeared from my life.

Underneath my bed turned out to be my sanctuary, especially when I would try desperately to block out my mother and father screaming at each other when he would return home from work some afternoons. When my father would come back after work, he would pick me up and hug and kiss me. On the days when they would fight, I remember mum throwing ceramic plates, cutlery anything she could get her hands on, aiming them directly at my dad's head. As he would duck the flying dishes, they would like wiz past his head and smash against the wall. I would run to my room and frantically crawl under my bed, crying and covering my ears.

The screaming voices turned to angry muffles as I would press my hands harder against my ears to drown out the noise. After a while, it would stop. I would slowly take my hands off my ears, waiting for silence. I would hear Dad leave the house, slamming the front door behind him. I would listen to Mum, crying. And wait for silence, then slowly and carefully venture out from under my bed – the dark enclosed space where I felt the safest.

I never understood why mum was so volatile towards my father. As an adult talking to my older sister Christine, I found out that mum had anger problems. While the doctors struggled to regulate mums antiseizure medications, she would have violent outbursts. Mum's violent outbursts resulted in her being admitted into the psychiatric hospital for weeks. Hearing that mental health issues run in the family would eventually help me to understand that my own mental health issues could be hereditary.

After my parents divorced, I never saw my father, living a chaotic life with my mother for the next twelve months. We ended up living with my grandparents in their red brick three-bedroom home in Doveton, at the time a low socio-economic suburb near Dandenong in the southeast of Melbourne. During the haphazard year with my mother, she met a man named Craig. Craig was a tall skinny man with brown hair and brown eyes, he would have been around thirty years old, and my mum was twenty-nine. I was three-and-a-half at the time and my mum and I lived in a caravan park with Craig in Chelsea. I had a Humphrey B Bear night light, which I loved, and he would comfort me as I feared the dark. When my parents were together, I loved watching Humphrey B Bear on TV.

One night, mum forgot to turn it on for me, and I slept at the front of the caravan while mum and Craig slept in the back with the sliding door shut. I asked mum to come to turn on my night light.

"I'll be there in a minute" she called.

"I need him on now, mum."

When she didn't come, I started to cry, feeling scared and anxious. I started yelling.

"I need my night light on - please!"

Craig shouted from their bed 'Shut the fuck up!"

As I started to get louder and more hysterical, Craig came crashing out of their room, holding a pillow in his hand and shoved it over my face. I remember kicking and pulling at his arms, but he was too strong. I couldn't breathe. I could feel the panic increase, my heart beating faster. I thought I was going to die. Then suddenly, I could breathe again. Mum pulled Craig off me shouting.

"Get the fuck off my son!"

Craig had pushed her, and she fell against the caravan door, hitting her head. As he attempted to put the pillow back over my face, she quickly got up and pushed him away from me.

"What the fuck is wrong with you, he's only three!"

Craig's face was red with anger as he screamed back.

"Get your fucking kid and get the fuck out of here before I kill him!"

Mum wrapped me in a blanket, and we left. Mum had called Uncle Theo from the Shell service station across the main road, and he came and picked us up. He wanted to go and bash Craig, but mum begged him not too. Uncle Theo dropped mum and I back at Nanna and grandpa's house, and we were safe again.

My grandparents' house would be where I would live for the next few years. Mum would come in and out of my life, leaving my Nanna to raise me like she had done with my sister Christine, who was fifteen at the time. Mum just couldn't be alone. She always had a new boyfriend and would go live with them until they got sick of her. Then Mum would return to my Nanna and grandpa's house. This would be a pattern over the next few years. Mum would come back and turn the house upside down like a tornado and then leave her wreckage behind. Bernice would try and be a mum to us, make promises she couldn't keep and when it became too hard for her or she found another boyfriend she would be off again; leaving Nanna to pick up the pieces with Christine and me.

Baby Shane Bautista

# CHAPTER 3

# THE MATRIARCH

I loved Nanna and Pop dearly. Their house was a small three-bedroom red brick home with a large backyard with two large plum trees. At the back of the house was a bungalow that was made up into an extra bedroom. I imagined that was where my uncle Robert (my mum's older brother) stayed when he was a teenager. I didn't meet him until I was an adult and now lives in Darwin.

Before moving up north, he had married my Aunty Margaret and together they had my cousin Sherrie. Sherrie was a few years older than me. Uncle Theo, sixteen at the time, met my Aunty Kerry when she was fifteen when he was working as a sewing machine mechanic. Aunty Kerry and her family migrated to

Australia from Denmark when she was fifteen. In their twenties, they married and had my cousin Tania who was born six months before myself. A few years later came my younger cousin Leonie. This was my family.

Nanna was our rock. Nanna was the one to go to when you needed a cuddle. Whenever I was sick and throwing up in the toilet, I would cry out for her, "Nanna! Nanna!" and she would be right there, rubbing my back and reassuring me that everything would be OK. When I was 4 years old and would wet the bed, she would never be angry.

She would just change the sheets and in her soothing tone would say, "We'll get it right next time darling, accidents happen". She would never make me feel shame or embarrassment. Nanna made me feel safe and loved always. She had raised my older sister Christine since she was a baby. Every Sunday we would all get together for the traditional Sunday roast. I would always help Nanna in the kitchen. She would always bake cupcakes in the morning, and I would lick the spoon and bowl of left-over cake mixture and end up with chocolate all over my face. These are my favourite memories.

My Nanna and pop, Betty and Charlie Wakefield departed England on the 26th June 1956, travelling on the ship called the 'S.S Orontes' and migrated to Australia with their three children, my mother Bernice, her twin brother Theo who were aged two and their older brother Robert who was four years old at the time.

Nanna had high expectations for her children, sending Bernice and Theo to tap dancing, singing, piano and acrobatic classes. Lessons and competitions took up their free time. I guess that is where I got my creative talent from. Nanna was a strong-willed lady. She was warmed natured but set in her ways and beliefs. She was a firm believer that you must always be polite, well-mannered and treat others the way you would like to be treated. If she were still here, I know that she wouldn't have cared that I was gay. If I was safe and happy, then that's all that would have mattered. Nanna cherished her family and proud of her children no matter how many mistakes they made. She adored her grandchildren always, tending to Christine and my needs before her own.

When my mother and Theo turned fourteen, mum rebelled and discontinued her lessons. Theo continued them for another year before quitting himself. My mother started to go off the rails. She was a beautiful girl with long black hair. Her looks would often get her the attention of the local boys, which resulted in her early sexual experience at just fourteen. Mum was attracted to guys a few years older than her.

When she was fifteen, she became pregnant to a local boy around seventeen years old. She was hoping he would marry her, but her dreams were shattered when he split. He never stuck around to see the pregnancy through or to meet his little girl, Christine Wakefield, born 18th January 1968. My mother had epilepsy her whole life, and as a teenager, her epilepsy was hard to control. She was prescribed strong anti-epileptic medication to attempt to control the seizures, she was used as a guinea pig by the doctors testing different drugs. As a result of her epilepsy, she received an invalid pension, Nanna helped raise Christine.

At this stage, their older brother Robert had moved up to Darwin to live when he was eighteen, and my mother and Theo didn't have much contact with him. Ten years after Christine was born, mum married soon after she met a thirty-two-year-old Filipino man who had arrived in Australia illegally, my father, Reynaldo Bautista. I was born on the 21st of June 1978. According to Christine, they seemed happy for a few years after they were married. When I read my foster care file years later, my social worker at the time said that my father married my mother so he could stay in the country.

Just like with her own kids, Nanna had ambitions for Christine and me. She sent us to ice skating lessons at the local rink in Dandenong. Christine had a few years of skating on me as I'd only starting skating when I was five years old, and Christine was now fifteen. I loved watching my sister skate. She was so elegant and graceful on the ice but also had some sass.

I have a memory of the Christmas show, and Christine did a routine to 'Eye of the Tiger' by the band Survivor. I remember watching her in awe, hoping I could be that good someday. But for now, I was dressed in a bunny suit skating around with the other five-year-old beginner skaters throwing Santa Chocolates into the crowd.

Through my darkest hours, I would always retreat into these memories, it would bring me comfort to know that once I felt love, acceptance and a true sense of belonging. I miss my Nanna and Pop. There's something special about grandparents. They filled the gap, and I didn't even mind that my mother and father weren't around so much because I had a love of my grandparents. To this day, when I think of them, I get a nostalgic feeling, a combination of sadness and warmth in my heart. I did once have a normal family environment, I just wished it could have stayed like that forever.

I had no idea she was sick. She was a strong woman and the matriarch of our family. The one person who offered me comfort and who showed me real love *was dying*. Christmas 1984, Nanna was admitted into the hospital due to a collapsed lung. Nanna was a heavy smoker, and during her hospital admission the doctors discovered her liver was riddled with cancer, and her prognosis was not good, giving her only 2-3 days before she would die.

Nanna used to go to her GP regularly so Christine and Pop couldn't understand how they had just discovered this now. Maybe Nanna knew and didn't say anything as she didn't want the fuss, or she didn't know. It's a question that will never be answered. Nanna went into the hospital and never came out. My life was about to change forever; the day I set foot into the hospital where my Nanna breathed her last breath, leaving all of us behind in a world that couldn't function without her.

Christine was so angry; she didn't want the doctors telling Nanna about her liver cancer's prognosis without our uncles being there. She was only Seventeen, and her voice didn't matter, it was Pop's decision, and he gave permission for the doctors to tell her. Christine called Uncle Robert in Darwin to tell him the news, and he rushed to get on the next flight to Melbourne.

Mum was uncontactable, and Uncle Theo was at his holiday house up at Walkerville, a coastal town 3 hours from Melbourne, with his family, and they didn't have a telephone in the holiday house. Christine called to local Police to find him, and when they eventually told him the bad news, Nanna was dying. She looked around the room for her kids, and they were not there. Unfortunately, Nanna's children never got to say goodbye.

As I entered her room, you could smell that distinct hospital smell, the mixture of hospital food, disinfectant and sick people. I was shocked to see my Nanna lying in her bed looking so pale, struggling to breathe, even with the oxygen mask on her face. I stood near the door to her room looking at a lady lying in the bed that didn't resemble the warm, loving face I knew.

She looked cold, weak and helpless as she gasped for the oxygen coming into the mask around her face. Nanna noticed me standing there in the distance and ushered me to come closer. At first, I hesitated scared and confused as to what was happening. Christine was standing next to her side, holding her hand, and Nanna pushed Christine's hand away and ushered me into her room with her hand. As I strolled over towards her bedside, she grabbed my hand and squeezed it tight, and that's when I knew that something was terribly wrong.

She took off her mask and whispered, "Nanna's going to heaven". I could feel the tears roll down my face and my throat tightening as I started crying hysterically, "No, Nanna please don't go! I don't want you to leave me!" She pulled me in closer to her, tears streaming down her face, and in-between gasps of air said, "Nanna loves you, look after Pop for me." These were her last words to me.

She then started to frantically gasp for air, her face white as a ghost. Her grip on my hand became stronger and firmer as she looked into my eyes. I could feel her panic, see it in her face. I was frightened, but I tried to stay brave for her. I was about to lose the one person that really loved me, who cared for me, the matriarch that kept the family together. I might have only been six years old, but I understood what we were all losing.

A nurse rushed into the room and tried to escort me outside, but I wouldn't let go, I clung onto Nanna's hand determined to not let go.

"NO! I want to stay with Nanna!"

The nurse finally loosened my grip and suggested that I come with her to do her rounds of the other patients. Christine and Pop encouraged me to go - *I reluctantly obeyed.* The elderly patients loved seeing me. One elderly lady gave me a hug and gave me a large bag of lollies. This started to take my mind off my Nanna's struggle for her life in the next room. Now a mental health nurse myself, I understand why the nurse removed me from Nanna's room. No little boy should see such a traumatic end to his beloved Nanna's life. As we headed back, I rushed back to show Nanna the bag of lollies, but I was too late.

As I watched the nurses pull the white sheet over my Nanna's lifeless body, I felt rage build up inside of me. Christine was crouched in the hallway wailing hysterically. Being eight months pregnant at the time the nurses were thinking of sedating her but didn't want to risk the pregnancy. I felt cheated, angry that I didn't get to say goodbye. I started to push through them.

"I want to see Nanna!" I cried.

Attempting to force my way through the nurses, I felt a hand grab the back of my t-shirt. I turned around and looked up at my pop.

"Come here, son."

As he pulled me in closer to him, I hugged him tightly, sobbing. My grandparents loved me dearly, *I knew that.* Nanna provided me with the stable, nurturing environment I needed. She was a positive influence in my life. I had no other significant relationship with anyone other than Nanna and Pop. Now she was gone.

My Pop, Nanna, Dad, Mum and
Sister Christine – Christmas Day

(Before I was born).

# CHAPTER 4

# SEX GAMES

**Aaron**

I was only six years old, and already, I had lived a chaotic life. Other children at school seemed to have a normal childhood, a childhood that I was robbed of during my developmental years. After Nanna died, the stable, nurturing environment that she had always tried to give me withered away with the autumn leaves. Pop seemed to enjoy his single life, or maybe it was his way of coping with his grief.

He would go to play bingo, attend dances and it didn't seem like that long after Nana died that he had a new girlfriend. Pop didn't know how to care for my needs. He would just eat when he was hungry and so would only feed me when he was hungry. As a result, I often attempted to cook my own food, which ended in me burning myself on the stove one night. Christine, now seventeen, had moved in with her boyfriend Pat who was twenty, at his mother's place across the road. Pat had three younger siblings, Rick eighteen, Aaron sixteen, and Amanda fifteen.

I didn't have friends of my own age, so I would hang around Amanda and Aaron mostly. Amanda had a horse, and she would take me horse riding with her. Amanda became like another big sister to me. Amanda was a good-looking girl with shoulder blade length brown wavy hair. She was a rebellious teenager, a tough girl that didn't take shit from no one. I liked that about her, and she would always look out for me.

Amanda would hug me when I missed Nanna and would let me cry on her shoulder and would tell me that it was OK to cry and miss her. I would often hang out at her place and became close to her older brothers. I started to develop a boyhood crush on Rick and Aaron. Rick and Aaron both had short spiky brown hair, masculine features and muscular bodies. Before getting to know these boys, I didn't have any real male role models apart from Pop who was absent and uncle Theo, who I would only see every so often.

One afternoon I went over to see if Christine or Amanda was home. I knocked on the front door, and Aaron answered.

"Hey, little man" Aaron said.

"Is my sister or Amanda home?" I enquired.

"Nah no one's home, but wanna hang out?"

"OK," I smiled and went inside.

Aaron took me into his bedroom, and we lay on his double bed and watched some music videos on his TV that he had recorded on his video recorder from last Sunday's Rage music video show on ABC. Aaron was lying there with no t-shirt on wearing only tracksuit pants. Aaron had a muscular body and smelt like rose washing detergent. He looked over at me and asked me something.

"Have you played mummies and daddies before?"

"No" I replied.

 "Want me to show you?" Aaron smiled.

"Sure" I said enthusiastically.

"Hop on top and lay on me". I climbed on top of Aaron as he instructed. I was a lot smaller than him, and my eyes were in line with the nipples on his chest. He pushed me down, so our penises were touching through his tracksuit pants. I could feel how hard and large he was, and I started to feel something that I hadn't felt before. My penis started to get hard.

"Now start rubbing up and down" Aaron ordered. I started to move my hips up and down, rubbing myself on him. It felt nice, I hadn't felt this feeling before, this electricity running through me and this strange feeling of pleasure that I didn't really understand. Aaron had his eyes closed, and his breathing became more rapid and more profound as he started to move his hips as well.

Aaron grabbed my bum with his hands and pressed me harder on top of him as his hips began to move faster. He began to groan. Then Aaron suddenly flipped me over and suddenly lying on top of me. The weight of his body was crushing me. His hips started to move faster, and his breaths become more rapid then suddenly, Aaron made a loud groaning noise, and his face looked like he was in pain! When he finished, Aaron rolled off me and lay next to me on his bed.

"Don't tell anyone about our game, OK? It's just for us" he said.

"No, I won't" I replied.

"I mean no one, not even Amanda or Christine" Aaron ordered.

I promised him I would keep our mummy and daddy game a secret. When we were alone in his house, we would play our secret 'mummy and daddy' game. I didn't really understand this game, but I was getting attention. Aaron was kind to me so I just let him do whatever he wanted to me, scared that if I said no Aaron wouldn't be my friend anymore. One time I was rubbing myself on top of him, and we heard the front door close and footsteps walking down towards his room. His door was ajar, and as it opened, Aaron pushed me off him, and I fell on the floor. Amanda popped around from behind the door.

"What are you guys doing?"

"Just hanging out. Shane was laying on the bed, and he fell off!" Aaron and I started laughing.

"Shane you're so clumsy" Amanda laughed.

"I know" I laughed back, picking myself up off the floor.

Amanda suggested we go over and to my house so I could ask Pop for some money to get fish and chips for dinner. As we left, Aaron yelled out "get me some dimmies and chips!" Pop gave me a 20 dollar note and Amanda and I walked up to our local fish and chip shop.

**Deano**

Christine's best friend Pam, who was also 18 years old lived next door to me, and when Pop was out of a night, she would come over and babysit me. Some nights she would come over to my place, or I would go over to her home. Pam lived with her mother and her younger brother Deano, and like me, they didn't have any contact with their father either. Aaron had a new girlfriend from school, so I didn't see him much, and our secret game had stopped as he wasn't home alone much anymore.

I had a new crush. I developed feelings for Deano, and I knew that I didn't have those kinds of feelings towards girls. I didn't understand the senses; they were just there. Deano was sweeter to me then Aaron was, we would ride our bikes up and down the street and play with his racing cars in his room.

One Saturday afternoon pop had gone out with his new girlfriend Mary to watch a movie and Pam was watching me over at her place. I was playing with Deano and his cars in his bedroom. Their mum was out that night, so it was only us three. Pam had to go to the shops to buy stuff for dinner and asked Deano to watch me as she wouldn't be more than an hour.

"I'll get us roast chicken and chips for dinner" she called out.

"OK, cool" Deano replied.

Pam left, and I heard the turning of the key as she locked the door behind her. Deano was a tall 13-year-old teenager with blond short spiky hair and a masculine build. At his high school, he was into basketball and played competition under 14's for Doveton. I was always fascinated with his muscular body, which would bulge out of his singlet tops. Deano paid me a lot of attention, more than Aaron did. Aaron only saw me when he wanted to play mummies and daddies. Deano was different. He made me feel special like I was a part of some-thing. It felt like a special friendship, a close bond that I felt with no other guy. We continued playing with his cars on his bedroom floor, then Deano stopped moving his car.

"Want to play another game, playing cars is getting boring" he asked.

"Sure" I said agreeably.

Deano stood up from the floor and closed his bedroom door then lay back on his bed. Oh, he wants to play mummies and daddies like Aaron, I thought to myself.

"Want to suck me?" Deano asked.

"How?"

Deano pulled his basketball shorts down and pulled out his erect penis. His penis was different from Aarons; Deano was circumcised, and Aarons had skin foreskin. I didn't know the difference then, but I found out later in my teenage years. Deano started giving me directions.

"Grab it with your hand and start pulling and then put my dick in your mouth and suck it like a lollipop."

I did what he asked I put the tip in my mouth and started sucking. Deano pushed my head down a little further onto his penis, moving it in and out of my mouth. I remember my eyes watering as he drove his penis further down my throat, almost making me gag.

"Come on don't stop" Deano pleaded. So, I kept going. Deano was always clean and smelt like fresh soap, and his clothes were washed in lavender washing powder. Deano started pulling himself faster while my mouth was over the head of his penis.

"Use your tongue" Deano instructed.

Then he started moaning and then pushed me away as he squirted his cum all over his chest -*I knew what that was coz*

*Aaron taught me.* Deano would often come over even when pop was home watching TV in the lounge room. Pop was never the same after Nanna died, and his hearing became worse so Pop would have the TV volume loud so he could hear it.

He couldn't hear any noises coming from my bedroom down the hall. Deano would lay on my bed, and I would suck his penis until he came. We would do this often at his house, at my house, and once we did it in his garden shed in the back yard when Pam and his mum were home. Deano sexually abused me for about six months.

It wasn't until I was 14 that I realised that I had been sexually abused at the age of six. Two guys that I trusted, looked up to, even loved. They both used me for their own sick pleasure! These guys wouldn't have realised or cared how this would affect me or my interactions with men later in life. At the age of six, I thought this was normal, I thought this is how you show love and how to keep a friend around. It's not right. It's abuse. My innocence was taken from me, and I didn't get a choice. I didn't have anyone to tell that would listen, so I guess I was an easy target.

Is this why I ended up so promiscuous when I came out and lived the Melbourne Gay scene? I grew up not feeling any self-worth or respect for myself, so I would just have sex with guys, thinking that this would end up into a caring, loving relationship, or end up on the other side of the spectrum and have a fear of commitment. The two boys who molested me added to the difficulty I had forming solid male relationships.

In my twenties when I came out, I would either become too needy with guys I tried to date or was promiscuous having random one-night stands with a lot of different men who slowly developed into an addiction. Needing that fix of some sort of connection through instant sexual gratification. I became a *male slut* as my friends at the time used to jokingly call me. I might have come across that way, but what I really was desperately trying to find was someone to love me.

# CHAPTER 5

# ABANDONED

It was clear my mum had abandoned Pop and me. After losing Nanna, mum had promised her twin brother that she would move back in with pop and I and help look after us both. That lasted two days and then she left to live with her new boyfriend Brian in Noble Park. She left Pop to struggle to look after a street smart, head-strong six-and-a-half-year-old that practically did what I wanted when I wanted.

Pop struggled to cope with looking after himself, let alone me, and couldn't handle the daily chores Nanna had always done. He was unable to make sure he was home when I came back from school each day or to make sure I was adequately clothed and fed. I was very street smart for a kid my age.

I could walk myself to school, which was only a fifteen-minute walk, but I had to cross the main road at the end of our street, which I did with ease. When Nanna was alive, she would make sure I have dressed appropriately, homework done, breakfast was eaten, teeth brushed and had my lunch box packed each day. Now she was gone pop wasn't so diligent. I guess he thought I could do it all myself.

My pop, Charles Wakefield, could be best described as an aging rogue. He liked to be called 'Charlie'. Pop liked to wear short shorts and t-shirts that had amusing messages on them during the summer. He had an eye for the ladies and was extremely vain. I remember him always making sure his grey hair and mustache were trimmed perfectly.

He would use Brylcreem to style his hair in a slicked back look. Brylcreem was popular with lads in the UK, and I guess he had always used it when he was a young lad himself. It was a brand he trusted. On a sunny Sunday afternoon, Charlie liked to wear nothing but his leopard print speedos as he mowed the front lawn for all the neighbours to see.

I loved my pop dearly, and I know he loved me. Pop just couldn't look after me the way Nanna did. He didn't under-stand the needs of a six-and-a-half-year-old. Charlie had never involved himself with the care of his own children and left Nanna to do all the work, which she didn't seem to mind. She never complained and took her job as a mother and grand-mother seriously.

My father started to come back on the scene, visiting me at Pop's house. My father didn't think he could care for me adequately, so he made an agreement with Pop to pay $15 a week child maintenance. Dad was often late with the payments which angered Pop. Pop's negative attitude obviously had rubbed off onto me as one weekend when my dad had come to see me, I had climbed on top of the house with a box of rotten tomatoes. As my dad stepped out of his car wearing a white, knitted jumper, I hailed rotten tomatoes at him. As they splattered all over his white jumper, I yelled at him.

"Give pop his money ya fuckin tight arse or fuck off!"

Just like when mum would throw dishes at my dad when they would fight, here was my dad trying to duck and weave away from the hurling tomatoes coming his way. He then gave up and got back into his car and drove away. Pop started laughing as he shouted, "Shane get down from there!" For dinner that night, Pop took me to McDonald's in Dandenong. I guess it was my reward.

There were days where I would go to school without my underpants on, just wearing my tracksuit pants, a t-shirt and hoodie, or I'd be wearing shoes with no socks. Other days I had no lunch. The teachers at my primary school and other kids parents from the local community were expressing concern at the care given to me by my grandfather.

These concerns were expressed to a social worker named Wendy, who worked at the Doveton Community Centre. In March 1985, Wendy notified Foster Care Westernport, a foster care agency (now Oz Child). Wendy was in her late forties and was a kind and warm lady that spent a lot of the time mediating between my family members on what was best for me.

Charlie acknowledged that he was not capable of caring for me properly. Nanna was the one who cared for my pop, Christine and me. Charlie didn't have any idea of what the needs of a six-and-a-half-year-old were. He had a new girlfriend and an active social life. When Pop went out at night, Christine,

Pam or Christine's boyfriend Pat's younger sister Fiona would take turns looking after me.

On the weekend or weeknights when Pop was out socialising Deano would sometimes volunteer to look after me when Fiona was busy, and Christine had her hands full with a new baby. Before Pam and Deano moved to Hastings after their mother passed, he would come over to 'babysit', and he would want to play our secret game.

He would come over most nights and lay on my bottom bunk bed while he made me suck his penis. I couldn't recall exactly how long this happened, but I know it was for at least a good six months. I was six-and-a-half-years-old when Deano's mum became ill, diagnosed with cancer. I didn't see Deano much during this time, and after three months their mum passed away. Deano and Pam went to live with relatives in Hastings, and I never saw Deano or Pam again.

It was the 3rd April 1985, and a family meeting was held at the Dandenong Family Court. I was not present, but Pop, Mum, Dad, Christine, Uncle Theo and Aunty Kerry were. According to my court case file, the meeting was filled with hostile parties. Everyone was angry at Mum, especially Christine and Uncle Theo, who felt Mum had broken her promise and had left Pop to look after me. Uncle Theo seemed upset and frustrated with the situation.

He was hurt and angry that Mum and Christine did not move back in with Pop to help look after us. He felt that he was always taking care of the family. When Uncle Theo started working as a sewing machine mechanic at the age of 16, he had no idea how to handle money and spent nearly everything he had. When he met Kerry, and after they married, Kerry taught Theo about budgeting, and they brought their first home in Doveton. They paid the house off quickly and sold it, giving them the finance to buy their large comfortable home in Endeavour Hills.

Uncle Theo was the success story of the family. He had a full-time job, was married, owned his own home in upper-class Endeavour Hills, and had two beautiful girls. He had paid for Nanna's funeral as Nanna and Pop had no money at all. Robert offered to pay half, but Theo never received any money from him. On occasion, Mum, Nanna and Pop would go to Uncle Theo for small loans until their pension cheques were due.

Uncle Theo felt a great deal of responsibility towards his family but felt used and angry that Pop could spend large sums now on clothes and not offer to reimburse him at all. There was also a lot of anger towards Mum for walking out on Pop and me just after Nanna's death. Uncle Theo told my social worker Wendy, that my Mum had told him she didn't want anything to do with me.

In the Family Court, Wendy explained to the family:

"This meeting aims to decide the best possible placement option for Shane."

In the room, you could cut the tension in the air with a knife. Uncle Theo started by saying, "Things have been handled poorly! I have always wanted to care for Shane, but I've been criticised for playing God!"

No one else said anything, and everyone was silent, then after a few minutes, Mum spoke, "I can't cope with Shane! I don't want or love him! I can't cope having Shane long term."

"I would love to take Shane, but I'm living in chaotic circumstances myself, caring for my one-month-old son Lee and I don't think I'm the best choice" Christine said. Christine then turned to Mum and abused her, "Mum you promised to look after Shane and Pop after Nanna died! You're the most selfish person I know! Don't you think you should start taking responsibility for your kids? You just do what you want!"

"I have an illness, and I can't cope!" Mum yelled back.

"Not a good enough excuse Mum, your epilepsy is managed with medication" Christine sniped back.

Wendy suggested that it may be a good idea if I lived with Uncle Theo and Aunty Kerry because out of the family, they could provide me with the best stable environment.

"Kerry is not sure about having Shane long term" Uncle Theo said.

"I need to have some time to think through some of the issues that could arise by bringing Shane into the family. Also, there is Tania and Leonie to consider, I would like to speak to them first" Aunty Kerry explained to Wendy.

Dad did not seem keen on the idea, even though he couldn't look after me himself.

"You hit Shane! There was a yellow streak down his back the last time you visited him!" Uncle Theo yelled.

"Shane was throwing rotten tomatoes at me from the roof of Charlie's house! That boy needs discipline! I'm going for full custody, and I'm getting a solicitor!" Dad said.

"Good luck with that mate!" Uncle Theo said.

My father, Rey, applied for sole custody. However, the courts found that Rey would not be a suitable caregiver for me then as we didn't have a father-son bond and he hadn't seen me much after mum, and he was divorced. Rey was granted regular access rights. He signed me over to the foster care system, managed by Foster Care Westernport.

Aunty Kerry's main concerns were that having three children would put a strain on them financially and that I would become the 'middle child.' As Tania and I were close in age (Tania being six months older), she felt this may make Leonie feel left out. However, she did think me being male might be better in this situation. Tania and Leonie, for their part, were excited to have me live with them.

Uncle Theo and my father had settled their differences, and it was decided that my Uncle and Aunt would be my new foster parents. They wanted the foster agency to stay involved to act as a mediator if any issues arose. They also welcomed the foster carer's allowance to assist with clothing and school fees for me. Rey was to continue paying them $15 per week child support.

My mother had utterly given me up, the woman who carried me for nine months, gave birth to me, protected me from that arsehole Craig trying to suffocate me. Now she had rejected me. She didn't feel that special bond between mother and son when she looked at me, she just saw something holding her back from life. Her rejection would soon come to taunt me growing up, giving me abandonment issues, developing detachment disorder as a child and a young adult.

# CHAPTER 6

# NEW FAMILY

Friday 19th April 1985, I remember sitting on the edge of the Kitchen table distraught as I was told that I couldn't live with Pop anymore and I was going to live with my Uncle Theo, Aunty Kerry, Tania and Leonie. At the time, I didn't really have a relationship with them as I had hardly seen them over the years. Uncle Theo was thirty-three years old at the time and was very serious and strict with his rules. I feared him when he got angry at us kids. He never smacked us, but when he yelled, you knew you were in trouble.

Uncle Theo was a strong male role model in my life, something I never had before, which brought about challenges as I was so used to wandering the streets on my own at my grandfather's, and their restrictions took a while to get used to. Uncle Theo loved me like one of his own, and when I lived with them, he spent a lot of time showing me guy things like a real father would. If you looked at our family, now dysfunctional without Nanna, I don't blame him for being this way.

He seemed to carry a lot of weight on his shoulders and felt a huge responsibility for his family – and now me as well. He carried around hurt and resentment, especially with my mother, Uncle Robert and Pop. Uncle Theo used to hate it that Pop could afford to buy new clothes but never had money for the necessities to take care of me.

"You will get to be our brother now!" Tania said in her mothering tone even though she was only six months older than me. I started to settle, and I began to warm to the thought of living with my cousins. At least I would be away from Aaron's mummy and daddy games and Deano's cock!

The Social worker Debra described Tania as a petite, beautiful, articulate little girl aged seven and in Grade Two who was very comfortable relating to adults, enjoys school and loves seeing members of her extended family. Tania thought that having me a part of the immediate family was terrific. Leonie was two years younger, and Debra described her as a blonde, brown-eyed bombshell. She loves kinder, and she too relates well to adults. Leonie said that she liked the idea of me living with them as I could teach her how to roller-skate.

Aunty Kerry was thirty-one years old and was born in Denmark. She migrated to Melbourne with her family when she was fifteen. Aunty Kerry had Danish schooling only however spoke English without an accent. She was an extremely bright, capable and warm person. Aunty Kerry was the eldest of four. Aunty Kerry's parents lived around the corner from us in Endeavour Hills. They were a close-knit, happy family who loved and supported each other. Aunty Kerry was very fond of her parents, especially her father, who was, in fact, her step-father. After Aunty Kerry mother's first marriage ended her mother remarried when Aunty Kerry was six years old. Kerry said she could not have picked a better father for her children.

When they all arrived in Australia, Aunty Kerry and her mother got machinist jobs in the same factory where Uncle Theo worked. They met each other when she was fifteen and a half years old. Debra described Kerry as a hard worker who still did machining at home in the garage workroom situated in the rear of the house to earn, as she put it, 'the jam.'

After a few months, I started to settle in and adjust to my new family. Aunty Kerry was always warm and kind to me, and I started to love living with them all. Aunty Kerry's family was a functional, loving, strong knit family, unlike my dysfunctional 'Wakefield' family.

On Christmas Eve, we would go to Aunty Kerry's parent's place, my new grandparents 'Mormor (Grandmother) and Morfa' (Grandfather). Danish Christmas happened on Christmas Eve and was a big family affair. Suddenly, I had new aunties and uncles and cousins, which I never had before. We would all sit around the table and eat a roast dinner of beef, pork and lamb with roasted potatoes and veggies.

For dessert, it was a tradition to have rice pudding, and mormor would place an almond in one of the large bowls, and if you got that almond, you would get a prize. At the end of dinner, the adults would place the Christmas tree in front of the lounge room, and we would hold hands as we walked around the tree singing Christmas carols.

Then the best part of the night that all of us kids were very excited about was, of course, the presents! When everyone arrived at the beginning of the night, the adults would place the gifts in a room on one of the beds. A few of the male adults would play Santa as us kids sat in a circle waiting with anticipation.

I lasted one year and six months with my aunt and uncle. In my foster care file, I found Debra's notes of home visits she made to Aunty Kerry, and Aunty Kerry said that I didn't quite fit in with the family and that the pressures of having a third child were too much financial pressure. Plus, I clashed with my younger cousin Leonie and because I was only six months younger than Tania, sometimes Leonie felt left out.

My time with Aunty Kerry and Uncle Theo was a positive experience for me as I gained stability, routine, family and started to enjoy my childhood status. Uncle Theo actively encouraged my Dad (Rey) to have regular contact with me so we could get to know each other. Rey started to have me over some weekends. My time spent with Rey was positive, and we began to enjoy each other's company when he turned up for access. Rey's lateness and last minute cancellations on occasions used to anger and frustrate Uncle Theo and Aunty Kerry as they found it hard to see my disappointment, plus it probably messed up their weekend plans as well.

My social worker Wendy had noted in my file that:

*Although Rey seemed enthusiastic about developing his relationship with his son Shane, Rey often seemed ambivalent, and sometimes failed to show up for his access. This would leave Shane disappointed, and Rey's inconsistent pattern of involvement in his son's life became an ongoing frustration for Shane's Aunt and Uncle, and the placement began to become stressed.*

With the financial and emotional pressures of having a third child to look after, Aunty Kerry and Uncle Theo thought it would be better if Rey took responsibility of me. My aunt and uncle put pressure on Dad to take me full-time. Even when he had not expressed any desire or confidence in his ability to care for me.

The 22nd of August 1986 was the day I was uprooted again and had to move on. I didn't understand why I had to move. *Did I do something wrong? Why didn't they want me to live with them anymore?* After a year and six months adjusting to the family routine, my school, and having Tania and Leonie as my siblings, I was going to be alone again. In my foster care file, it was recorded that '*Kerry found it hard to manage three children, and she didn't think I fitted into the family unit.*'

I was too young to fully understand and had learnt to adapt to constant changes in my young life. I began to learn that my living situation was never permanent. The thought of moving from place to place was always in the back of my mind. I left the four-bedroom house in Endeavour Hills, the family I knew for sixteen months and moved into a two-bedroom apartment in Dandenong, a lower socio-economic suburb 20 minutes away from my Aunt and Uncles; with a man I had only just started to get to know.

# CHAPTER 7

# NEGLECT

Dad wasn't ready to care for me full-time, but he felt the pressure from Uncle Theo and Aunty Kerry to take responsibility for me and felt that he thought he had no choice. At the time I was moving from my aunt and uncle's to my Dad's, Wendy attempted to explore his attitude towards providing for me on a full-time basis. Dad had given little thought to the practical demands of what it took to care for his seven-year-old son but was preoccupied and burdened with a sense of responsibility that left him no choice but to take me into his care.

I know my father obviously cared for me, but he had significant deficits in his parenting ability. Just the same as Pop, Dad had no idea of what the emotional or developmental needs of a seven-year-old were.

When Wendy would do house calls to see how we were going, Dad never liked the intrusion. To Wendy, it appeared that Rey provided the basic needs such as food, adequate clothing and shelter. However, she noted in her report that '*the environment provided for Shane is sterile and unstimulating where Shane's emotional needs have been neglected, and to an extent, the deprivation of his grandfather's care has resumed.*'

Dad had enrolled me to finish Term Four of grade Three at St. Mary's Primary School, a private Catholic school in Dandenong. Dad was working for the Heinz factory in Dandenong as a forklift driver. Heinz made anything from baby food, tomato sauce to canned spaghetti and baked beans. He would often bring home boxes of canned spaghetti and baked beans, and I would usually eat them on toast for breakfast.

I found it hard to make friends at school as I was the new kid coming into the end of the school year. I wasn't good at team sports, so I was shunned by the boys, and at the age of seven-and-a-half I wasn't welcome to hang around the girls, so I spent the lunch breaks by myself. I really missed Tania and our friends at Chalcot Lodge Primary back in Endeavour Hills.

I felt alone, and this is the first time I thought of killing myself, but I didn't know how. I never saw Aunty Kerry, Uncle Theo or Tania and Leonie for the entire time I spent living with my Dad, which was thirteen months in total.

Dad had a Filipino girlfriend named Susan, and she had a two-year-old boy called Pacco. Susan was kind enough, but I never bonded with her nor my father. Before she moved in with us, Dad would take me to her apartment on a Sunday, and we had to wait in the car around the corner until her ex-husband left when he would drop Pacco off after his weekend with Pacco. Susan's ex-husband was Italian, and he didn't know she was dating my Dad. We would wait while Dad plucked his grey hairs from his head looking in the rear-view mirror.

I hated it. I was so bored every time we had to see Susan. Susan and her son moved in for a few months, but the relationship didn't last that long after that and Susan and her son moved out.

Next door lived a lady in her sixties named Gale, who lived with her thirty-year-old son Jim. Gale was fit for her age and liked to take care of herself. She was English and had migrated to Australia when she and her late husband Bob in the 1960s. Even though her appearance was proper, it was contrary to her thick northern English accent. Bob had passed away 10 years earlier, from a heart attack.

Her only child Jim had a typical Australian accent and was very masculine and worked as a diesel mechanic. He didn't have a girlfriend, and he didn't appear to have many friends. He was a bit of a loner, looking after Gale like a good son. I liked him as he was always kind to me. Gale would have me over for dinner some nights when my Dad wasn't around. Gale would display her disgust towards my father and say to me, "What type of father leaves his seven-year-old son by himself at night?"

Gale took a liking to me, and I would earn pocket money by washing the oil stains from her carport sometimes, and she would pay me $10. As soon as I got paid, I would ride my bike down to the iconic music store Brashs in Dandenong's city centre. For those of you that grew up in Melbourne in the '80s and '90s, you'll all know what I'm talking about. Brashs had everything from Vinyl records, cassettes and CDs.

They even stocked pianos and other musical instruments. Remember that iconic Brashs TV commercial starring the *Sale of the Century host* Tony Barber and the catchphrase 'Where the answer is Brashs' at the end of the ad? I would buy the 45-inch singles on a vinyl record. I was very excited to buy the 1980's girl duo Mel and Kim's new single 'Respectable'.

On the days and nights Dad left me on my own I would feel scared and lonely. To entertain myself, I would dance around the lounge room to my music, pretending to be in a music video clip. When nightfall came, I would watch TV on the floor with my bowl of 2-minute noodles.

I remember the time that I felt the most scared was when the 1987 Grim Reaper AIDS commercial would come on. This commercial was part of an education campaign by the National Advisory Committee on AIDS (NACAIDS). The ad showed grim reapers playing ten pin bowling in a bowling alley knocking down grandmothers and grandfathers, mothers, fathers and children as though they were bowling pins. During this ad, I was so scared I would mute the TV and close my eyes and hide under the coffee table until it was over.

My sister Christine lived around the corner in a two bedroom flat with her two-year-old son, my nephew Lee. I would go over there some days to hang out with Christine and play with Lee. Sometimes I would skip school when Dad was away and hang around at Christine's house. I reconnected with Amanda again, Lee's father's younger sister who I used to hang around when I lived in Doveton with Pop. Amanda was around eighteen, unemployed and living off the dole. I would often go to her apartment on the weekends and sometimes during the week skipping school.

I was in Grade Four, and I didn't have friends at school anyway, so I would rather hang out with Amanda and her friends. Amanda hung out with a group of misfits that wore Metal Jackets in either army green or denim, with metal studs on the shoulders, and 80's band patches of Bon Jovi, AC/DC, Iron Maiden, Metallica and others sewn on them. We would go to the Nobel Park roller skating rink, and I would watch them headbang in front of the DJ booth to Jon Bon Jovi's 'Livin' on a Prayer'.

It was a Friday night at the skating rink and one of the girls, Jennie, was hammered, and as a group, we followed her over the road to the local primary school, which had a function in the school hall. On the side of the building were windows high up towards the roof. Jennie picked up a large rock and threw it up towards the windows, and as the rock crashed through the windows she yelled, "Betta fuckin' run bitches!" We all took off running down the side of the hall, jumping the school fence as three men started chasing us.

My heart was pounding out of my chest, but I loved the excitement of being a misfit. The freedom of doing what the hell I wanted, when I wanted to. Some of the gang split up while Amanda and a couple of the guys and I made it back into the skating rink. The men from the hall chased the others along the street. When we knew we were safe, we looked at each other and burst out laughing. I was seven going on seventeen, beyond my years. This would cause a problem later when I ended up in foster care with a family with structure and rules. When I was removed from my dad's care, I never saw Amanda again.

Wednesday the 16th September 1987 is the day I was removed from my father's care. I was walking home from school, and as I entered our apartment complex, I noticed a police car waiting out the front of our apartment. I went running as I thought they were here to arrest me because the week before I had been caught shoplifting food from our local supermarket, but the manager had let me go. A female and male copper reassured me that I wasn't in trouble.

"Hi, are you Shane?" the female copper asked

"Yes."

"I'm Sarah, and this is Jack. We're from the Community Policing Squad (CPS), Where's your dad?"

"I dunno he's out somewhere."

"Can we come in?"

"Yeah, OK."

I let them into the apartment, and they looked around, and the female copper looked in the kitchen cupboards to find a few packets of two-minute noodles in the cupboard, and in the fridge was only a bottle of water, a carton of eggs and a bottle of orange juice.

"What have you been eating for dinner?" the female copper asked. I shrugged my shoulders not saying anything.

"Have you been in a police car before?"

"No" I said as I shook my head.

"Well, today is your lucky day!" she smiled.

Sarah and Jack guided me up to my room to grab my backpack and pack some pajamas and a change of clothes. The two police officers drove me in their police car and to ease my anxiety, Jack put on the siren and lights for a bit. He looked back at me and smiled when he turned them off.

"Are you hungry mate?" Jack asked.

"Yes" I answered.

Jack drove through the McDonald's drive-through and ordered me a small cheeseburger meal. It came packaged in a plastic ship and had a toy inside. They were kind and made me feel at ease. I sat in one of the interview rooms and ate my Maccas meal. They must have called my Dad at work as I was there a couple of hours before he arrived. When Dad arrived at the station and went into the room where I had been waiting, he looked angry

"What have you done now!" Dad yelled

"It's not your son that's in trouble. It's you, Mr Bautista!" Sarah firmly said.

My Dad was in shock as he sat down at the other end of the table. Sarah explained to him that they received a complaint of childhood neglect from one of his neighbours. Apparently, Dad has been spoken to before by the CPS after concerns by the social worker, Barbara. Dad started to cry as he was informed that I would be removed from his care and placed in an emergency home. A court date will be set to determine my future, but I would be placed in foster care. Dad pleaded with them. I just sat watching this unfold, thinking, why does he want me? He's never home anyway. I was happy to be leaving him.

# CHAPTER 8

# ON THE MOVE AGAIN

The drive seemed to take forever in the dark of the night and without knowing the people I was about to meet; I couldn't help but feel anxious. When any child is taken away from their parents, the assumed reaction would be that they would cry and become emotional. That never happened to me. I never felt any of these when I was taken away from my Dad, but I did fear the unknown. What was going to happen to me? Where was I going? Although I was on edge, the consistent pattern of being moved around was typical for me. Seven years old and I was used to the inconsistency of my life. I had the thought that everything would be fine. I wouldn't need too many of my things as I wouldn't be staying where I was going too long.

The car came to a halt, and there I sat in the back of the police car, not knowing what to do next. The loud sound of dogs barking echoed through the night sky. As I stepped out of the car two large dogs were eager to meet me. I was surprised to find them so friendly as their barks seemed so threatening. "Oh, don't mind them they won't bite. Aaron! Chloe! Come here!" A female voice called the dogs away. Aaron was a large German Shepherd male, and Chloe was a mixed breed female. As I approached the front door, I was greeted by a lady in her forties.

"Hello, I'm Joan" she said, greeting me with a smile. Joan had a warm, friendly vibe and made me feel comfortable straight away. I arrived with nothing but my pajamas and a change of underpants and socks in my little backpack.

It was surreal walking into a strangers home and greeted by people I didn't know. Joan went around the lounge room, introducing me. Sitting on the armchair was Brian, Joan's husband, who was a policeman. Lying on the floor watching TV were two good looking, stocky teenage boys. Paul was seventeen years old and was working as a 1st-year mechanic apprentice, and Scott was fifteen years old and a Year 10 high school student. They turned to say hi and then reverted their attention back to the TV. Joan and Brian had fostered over three-hundred children in their time and receiving a child late at night in an emergency wasn't uncommon for them.

In 1966 Joan and Brian began their foster care journey when Joan noticed an advertisement to offer their home as a holiday destination for Aboriginal children from Queensland. The initiative was called the 'Harold Blair Aboriginal Children's Holiday Project.' Harold Blair was an Aboriginal man, singer and Aboriginal activist. Two Aboriginal children that had stayed with them are now in their fifties and keep in contact with us to this day. When Joan and Brian started fostering, they had twin girls of their own who were born in 1965 named Michelle and Leanne. In 1970 their son Paul was born, and in 1973 the youngest son Scott was born three years later. It was around 1980 when they started fostering through the foster care agency Foster Care Westernport, which is now known as Oz Child.

Ward number 101-6-759 was my identification in the Department and Human Services Child Protection database. The next day after being placed with the Graham family for emergency care, I went to the children's court. I was asked by the court social worker if I wanted to go back to my Dad's or stay with the Graham's. I told the court that the Graham's place was like a dream come true as they lived on a farm and had a lot of animals, and I would like to stay there. The Wardship case was adjourned for a couple of months. In the meantime, the Graham's were given a 'Safe Custody Order'. My placement with the Graham's was only for a short period as in a few months the family would be going on a holiday around Australia.

### 29/09/1987: Access with Shane and Rey 10:00hrs

*Rey was very subdued. Only made two comments to Shane, about school and his new shoes. Rey appears not to know how to relate to Shane. There seems to be no father/son bond. Shane settling too well into foster care after a year with his Dad, with no anger or sadness.*

*Driving Shane home after access, Shane confirmed that he and his dad didn't have much to say to each other. Shane talked about being left alone several nights at a time when Dad visited* *his girlfriend in the inner-city area. Shane's favourite memories, those living with his maternal grandmother before her death, and baking cakes with her. Shane loves being at the Graham's on the farm, appears to be enjoying his childhood status. Shane makes allowances for his Dad in a parentified way, "they probably do things differently in the Philippines." **Debra Cunningham – Social Worker.***

I had settled into my new surroundings and with the Graham family quite well. I felt safe although Joan said that I was like her little shadow. At home, wherever she went, I was right behind her. If she went outside to hang the washing, I'd follow to help her. When no one else was home, and I couldn't find her, I started to get anxiety, afraid that I was being left alone again. I began to get panicked and overcome with fear, then when I found her, my anxiety levels would drop, followed by a sense of relief. Rey kept changing his mind about whether to fight for my custody or not.

**29/09/1987: Visit with Rey 15:00hrs**
*First visit, Rey not sure which way to go. He agreed that it might be better for Shane to be with another family where he could visit and be a better part-time father.*

*Rey is in denial about leaving Shane and gave way to ambivalence about the whole situation. Before this visit, I had great difficulty contacting Rey, called and left five messages. Rey eventually returned my call in two days, and he did not make any attempt to visit the agency when his flat is only down the road from the agency.* **Debra Cunningham – Social Worker.**

***30/09/1987: Visit from Rey at my Request***

*Rey now wants to contest the case. Apparently, he has spoken to his Doctor brother in New York, America who feels Shane should stay within the family. Brother prepared to pay legal costs. Rey stated: "I have had a good family life. I want Shane to have the same. Shane was spoilt by his mother, wants to be both mother and father to Shane". Rey said he misses Shane dreadfully – "I nearly cried yesterday" – the place is lonely without Shane. Rey was concerned if he (Rey) was suddenly sick, as he suffers from high blood pressure and kidney disease, who would call the ambulance and look after him? Rey has spoken to his solicitor Julie Berry. Rey's sister in the Philippines along with his brother in Florida USA both have said that he should fight for Shane. **Debra Cunningham – Social Worker.***

With his meeting with Debra, he seemed very hard on himself. He agreed it was inexcusable to leave me alone by myself. However, he denied the number of times I was left alone, saying *"It was only occasionally"*. Rey was also concerned about my schooling and saying that it wasn't right for me to grow up outside of the family. I never met Rey's siblings, I didn't know anything about the Filipino culture, and Rey never taught me Tagalog, the Filipino language. This made it difficult when I would have access with Rey, and he would be around his friends, I just sat there not knowing what they were talking about. I really felt a disconnect from my culture – I had no culture. After a couple of court adjournments, two months later I was officially made a 'Ward of the State'.

***11/11/1987: Wardship Outcome***

*Shane was admitted to the care of the Department of Health &
Human Services on the 10/11/1987 at Springvale Court under
the reasons of "the guardian of or persons having custody or
responsibility for the child do not exercise adequate supervision
and control over the child or young person".* ***Debra Cunningham
– Social Worker.***

Rey never showed up to the court to contest the proceedings or to fight for me. None of my family did. Rey was uncontactable as he had gone back home to the Philippines for two and a half months to visit family. He gave up. He left Australia on the 18th of November 1987 and returned on the 5th January 1988.

***6/01/1988: Telephone Contact with
Mr Bautista & Christine Wakefield***

*The Social Worker (Debra) spoke with Mr Bautista regarding
Shane's future, and he was informed of the case plan meeting and
recommendation. Mr Bautista was quite happy for Shane to be in
foster care and stated he was pleased to have ongoing contact with
him on weekends.*

*The writer also spoke with Christine Wakefield (Shane's half-
sister) on two occasions concerning Shane's placement. Christine
says she is happy to visit Shane wherever he is placed and possibly
have Shane for occasional leave. The writer was unable to contact
Shane's Aunt and Uncle (Theo & Kerry Wakefield) at the time of
the report. However, the foster care staff has indicated that the
Wakefield's are aware of Shane being placed in foster care.* ***Debra
Cunningham – Social Worker.***

I spent Christmas with my new foster family, but I never heard from him or any of my extended maternal family that year. I had met the Graham's extended family that year. Brian's side (the Grahams) were a large family, and the older cousins were eager to welcome me into the family. I had a great Christmas that year. Surprisingly, I wasn't perturbed by my maternal family's absence. Either I was so used to changes in my life that I had developed some resilience or my brain disassociated from my entire traumatic childhood to date. Maybe both.

Before I was removed from Rey's care, the music teacher at school discovered I could sing. At the end of Term Four, St. Mary's put on a Christmas show that all year levels had to perform in. Our Grade Four class's show stopper was about a boy that must save the town by flying around the world to seek a wizard that could save the town from doom. The teacher auditioned the entire class of boys who were mostly tone deaf. I was the last of the boys to sing, '*Come fly away, in my beautiful, my beautiful balloon*'.

She seemed amazed, saying "Wow, Shane, you can sing!"

From that music class, I became the lead in our little musical number at eight years old. Joan and Scott (Joan's youngest son, 15 years old) came and watched me perform. Rey never showed -no surprise there! Joan asked me if I had ever acted before. I never did, this was my first time. "That was really good!" Joan said. Despite the number of times I missed school and the disruptions when I was removed, I still managed to receive mainly A's and B's for English, Maths, Art, Science and Sport for the second half of the year. At the end of the school year, 1987, I had left St Mary's Primary, and Joan enrolled me in Grade Five at Hampton Park Primary School, which was closer to the farm.

Before Christmas, Debra had left Foster Care Westernport and was replaced by a new Social Worker named Sarah Jackson. I was sad to say goodbye to Debra as she had been a part of the journey since I was five years old.

# CHAPTER 9

# SHIT FATHER

In January 1988 Rey became sick and was admitted into Burwood Hospital. He had a blood clot blockage in his aortic artery, which carries oxygenated blood to the brain and the rest of the body. The clot had moved from the artery near his heart, and he needed open heart surgery to remove the blockage. Sarah had phoned the hospital and was told by the nursing staff that the operation was a success and Rey was recovering well. Sarah called Joan to let her know the news and Joan took me to visit Rey that evening.

### 20/1/1988 Phone Call to Joan

*Rey was happy to see Shane and Joan. Shane was reluctant to go into seeing Rey but got more enthusiastic when Joan made up a basket of fruit to take in. Although Rey was talkative, there were still long silences between them. Shane started the conversation once or twice, telling Rey about the holiday to Darwin coming up. On the way home after the visit, Joan said, "I think your Dad was pleased to see you". Shane shrugged his shoulders and replied, "Oh Yeah, he might have been".*

*Joan talked to Rey about Shane's Schooling for this year. Rey took the attitude that "it was up to Joan." Joan told Rey that Shane is keen to go to Hampton Park Primary.*

*Joan will enroll Shane this coming year into Hampton Park Primary to commence grade five. Discussed with Joan the possibility of Shane staying long- term with the Grahams, over the next twelve months. Joan said this would be fine. She said the only problem she is having with Shane is that he is "lazy" and reluctant to do any household tasks. I suggested that perhaps she could give him 50 cents each week if he completed his tasks. Joan thought she would give this a try. Otherwise, there seem to be no problems, particularly if Shane starts school in Hampton Park and makes some local friends. He is terrified of being left alone.*

*Joan's main worry about having Shane long term is that they are too old for him as a family and the lack of suitable friends for him.* **Sarah Jackson – Social Worker.**

There was no father-son bond between my father and me. We didn't know how to relate to one another. When he became well enough to have me for weekend visits, I always left disappointed. Rey never spent quality with me, always brought me to his friend's house and would leave me to my own devices. When I went over during a few days of the school holidays, he noticed I had a bank book with me. Joan had started a bank account for me to encourage me to save the pocket money I got for completing my chores. Rey would take me into the bank and make me withdraw cash so he could buy cigarettes. When I told Joan, she was furious at Rey for using me like that. Joan suggested that I leave the bank book with her so Rey couldn't ask me for money next time I saw him.

*22/08/1988 Phone Call from Ambelle Bautista*
*Ambelle apparently is a half-sister of Shane. She last saw Shane last year in June and would like to see him again. She is living in North Balwyn in a boarding house but moving (doesn't know where to) soon. She sees Rey from time to time and is visiting him today in the hospital. Ambelle wanted to know how Shane was and where he was living.*

*I explained that he was a State Ward and was in long term placement with the Grahams. Told Ambelle that I would speak to Rey and Shane first about a possible meeting for her and Shane, maybe at Rey's when he gets home. Rey will let her know or will try and contact her when I have visited Rey and discussed it with him and Shane. (Not sure where this sister fits into the family situation)* **Sarah Jackson – Social Worker.**

I first met my half-sister from the Philippines a few months before I was removed from Rey's care. Ambelle was eighteen at the time and had moved to Australia to further her higher education studies and look after our father. She only lasted a few weeks, and I vaguely remember that Rey and Ambelle had a huge fight and she had walked out and never come back. Ambelle had lived with family friends and completed her business studies at a Tafe College Melbourne and ended up getting a job in sales. I never saw her much during that time.

What I do remember was that I loved having another big sister. I admired Ambelle. She came to another country to live with our father and have better opportunities that the Philippines couldn't provide, only to be disappointed by him and now fending for herself at eighteen. Christine and Ambelle had the courage and resilience to keep going when things were tough for them at such young ages. They hadn't met at that time yet, but they were two women in my life that I looked up to. Maybe that's where I got my survival instincts from and the resilience to bounce back from the shit I endured in my life.

At times I would feel sad and guilty for the anger I felt towards Rey, especially when he would get sick. In February 1988, Rey went into complete kidney failure resulting in another surgery to insert a tube from his urethra out of his abdomen, so he could self-perform dialysis every four hours by flushing his kidneys with saline fluid, and after a couple of hours the bag would fill up with urine. He was placed on a donor list. The wait for new kidneys could be two weeks or four years. Having just had heart surgery and then problems with his kidneys, Rey's recovery in the hospital took a few months.

*18/04/1988 Visit to Rey in Prince Henry's Hospital*
*with Shane*
*Spoke to Joan when I returned Shane home. We agreed we would see how Rey's health progresses before organising home access. Joan said that the placement is going well. Joan worries about Shane not fitting in with the family chores and taking himself too seriously. She agreed that these things take time – now that Shane knows he is not leaving the Grahams could make the difference.* **Sarah Jackson – Social Worker.**

When I was told I was staying for another twelve months, I was relieved not to be moving again. I still wasn't sure about the family dynamics, though. I tried to click with Scott, but he was fifteen nearly turning sixteen and we had nothing really in common. Scott would play with me sometimes, teaching me how to kick the footy in the back paddocks and how to fire the slug rifle shooting cans off the fence. Having a healthy relationship with an older guy seemed strange at first since my only experience in the past was of a sexual nature. After a while, I started to trust Scott and Paul and enjoyed having older brothers to teach me things as I grew up.

# CHAPTER 10

# BECOMING A PART OF THE FAMILY

I was starting to become more like one of the family. Brian and Joan, instead of putting me in respite care while they went away with the family to Darwin, decided to take me with them. When Joan and Brian were discussing the holiday and who would look after me, Brian had said "Why can't we just take Shane with us?" So, Joan asked my social worker to gain permission from the department of human health and services (DHHS). They granted the request, and I would be going around half of Australia with the Graham family from the 10th June to 9th July 1988.

Joan had attempted to arrange a visit with Rey before we left for Darwin. He had been discharged from the hospital the week before, and Joan thought it would be nice if I saw him before we went. I was apprehensive at first the thought of another visit with awkward silences and nothing much to say to each other. The same old questions about school and Rey talking about how sick he has been as his sickness now defined him, and he could use this as an excuse for being such a shitty father. I would be indecisive. One minute I would want to see him, and then I would change my mind once 'Mr Anxiety' had sat on my shoulder reminding me of all the reasons why it was a bad idea.

'Shane, you always get left alone. Your father doesn't give a shit about you, he only wants you there to call the ambulance in case he has a turn.' Mr Anxiety was relentless, and he was hard to turn off.


### 13/04/1988 Phone Call to Joan

*Joan organised for Shane to visit Rey Thursday (7th April). Shane reluctantly phones Rey himself on the Wednesday evening, after he had asked to see him the Saturday before. Joan was not happy when she arrived at Rey's last Thursday, he wasn't there. Rey had left for Prince Henry's Hospital at 9:00am that morning without calling Joan to let her know. Only Ambelle there. Shane was disappointed about not seeing his Dad.*

*There is some suggestion that Shane might have spent Easter at Rey's, but when given time to think about it and the choice of going to the Graham's beach house in Loch Sport, Shane chose to go to Loch Sport. Joan says that Shane relates well to her mother and opens-up to her. He told her last week, before Easter, 'I might be going to Dad's at Easter, but I'm a bit frightened about being left by myself'* **Sarah Jackson – Social Worker.**

I loved going up to the beach house. Paul had brought a speed boat and started teaching how to water ski. Surprisingly I picked it up fast, skiing on double ski's, and it wasn't long before I transitioned to a single ski (slalom skiing). I had been with the Grahams for nearly 5 months now, and I addressed Joan and Brian as Aunty Joan and Uncle Brian. They never had to worry about us going out by ourselves as Loch Sport was a quiet, safe place. Loch Sport was a thirty-minute drive from Sale located in the Gippsland Region of Victoria, taking only around 3 hours to drive there.

The beach house was next to the local Bakery, and I remember they had the best pies and hot jam doughnuts. Michelle and Leanne would buy them for us for lunch. Before then I hadn't tasted anything so good for a long time. We would water ski on the lake, and I thought I had hit the jackpot being placed with the Graham family.

I lived on a farm, with horses, cows, sheep, chickens, cats and dogs and holiday trips to our beach house. I had big brothers and sisters that treated me like their little brother as if they had known me from birth with foster parents that loved me. It was a far cry from where I had come from and for the first time in my young life, I felt happy and safe in my new environment. Finally, I might get the nurturing I got when my Nanna was alive.

A few months before we left for Darwin, Joan and Brian brought an 18-seater white bus for the trip. Paul was an apprentice mechanic, and he worked on the bus, so it was ready for the journey. Joan, Brian, Paul, Scott, Brian's parents (Nanna and Grandpa), cousin Tracey and two-family friends, Mr and Mrs Cochran, and I headed up the Northern Territory. A few days before we left, Paul had rolled his ankle at work and ended up in a fiberglass cast on his foot and ankle. He wasn't happy about that, but it didn't stop him from coming.

We traveled up through Adelaide and Coober Pedy, a town located north of South Australia, famous for its opal mining and underground residences called 'dug-outs' made due to the scorching daytime heat. Coober Pedy derives from the local Aboriginal name Kupa - Piti, which means 'boys waterhole'. The condition to have two months off school during June, July and some of August, was for me to keep a diary and write to the class of my experiences.

Driving along the Stuart Highway from Coober Pedy is a long stretch of highway that seems endless. Halfway between the South Australian border and Alice Springs were dead Kangaroos for two to three kilometers that had been most likely hit by road train truck at night. In one of my letters I had written and sent to my primary school class back in Melbourne, I had mentioned the dead Kangaroos along the highway. I must have given too much information about the blood and guts on the road because upon my return, the teacher said the classmates were grossed out but enjoyed my letter.

We had stopped at all the iconic Australian places like Uluru (Ayers Rock) and the Olgas in the red centre of Australia. Fortunately for us, our bus broke down in Mataranka Springs, and we stayed in paradise for the next seven days as we waited for an engine part to arrive from Darwin. Crystal blue, clear thermal spring waters surrounded by a tropical oasis set the serene scene of this untouched piece of heaven. By the time we left, Paul's cast had ended up a slither around the heel of his foot as he refused to not swim during our Mataranka stay and he ended up cutting the rest of the cast-off. When Joan questioned him about his foot, he would say "My foot's fine mum."

Our next stop was at Katherine, around three hours from Darwin. We set up camp for a few days, and I remember going to collect firewood with Paul, and he thought it would be funny to tell the eight-year-old me to watch out for buffalo as they chase you. As we were walking back, arms full of sticks for firewood Paul suddenly yells out "Shane Run! a buffalo's coming!" Dropping the bunch of sticks, I start running, terrified for my life thinking this big buffalo is going to kill us. Then I hear Paul cracking up laughing, then I realised he was joking. I stopped running and started laughing. "Oh, ya dickhead, I shit myself!"

The next day Scott, Paul and I went to try our luck fishing for barramundi in the Katherine River. Joan and Brain both warned us all, "Don't stand too close to the water's edge." The thing about up north is that the rivers are full saltwater crocodiles that can grab you in a split second and drag you into the river, never to be seen again.

This didn't deter three boys wanting to fish. We were only out fishing for ten minutes, and Scott had caught a barramundi! Excitedly reeling it in and almost bringing it to the bank of the river, it jumped off the line. "Oh, little bastard" Scott said. Then in the middle of the river, we saw the eyes of a croc rise from the water and then disappear into the river again. "Oh shit, we better go look at that croc!" Paul said.

We returned to the camp and Grandpa razzed us up about the Barramundi that got away. After a few days, we finally reached the top end's capital city of Darwin. I wasn't used to such hot sunny days and always spent most of the days in the pool to cool off. One afternoon Paul, Scott and I went into town with Grandpa, and he stopped into the pub to place a bet on the horses. While we waited out the front, we were sitting on a concrete block out the front of the pub. Stumbling down the stairs was an Aboriginal woman who was accompanied by a white fella. She looked like she was in her mid-thirties, and as the Aboriginal women stepped out the door, she stopped and looked at me. Suddenly, she pulled at my arms shouting, "You're my son! You're my son! Whitman takes you away from me!" As she attempted to pull me off the concrete block, I grabbed onto Paul with a look of fear in my eyes. "No! No, he's not your son, he's from Melbourne," Paul said to the woman. Grandpa came out to witness the commotion and said, "No love he's from Melbourne, let him go, hey."

The Aboriginal women let me go, looking saddened and confused and said, "You're my son's cousin!" The white fella that was with her pulled her away and ushered her down the street. This story was Grandpa's favourite story to tell at family gatherings, parties, anywhere as he saw the funny side in which in my first time up north, I nearly got kidnapped by an Aboriginal woman.

It wasn't until my own involvement with the Aboriginal community through my best mate Tom, who I had met at university and became like a brother to me, that I learnt about the stolen generation. Tom's mum was from the stolen generation, and the trauma that caused Aboriginal mothers, families and their communities were horrific.

When I now think of that Aboriginal woman back in Darwin, I feel such empathy and sadness at her grief of losing her son and then feeling the slight hope she must have felt when she mistook me for her stolen son, only to be traumatised again that her dream was shattered.

On the way back home, we cut across Queensland to Surfers Paradise to visit Brian's brother, Uncle Kevin, his wife Aunty Margret and cousins Darren and Craig. The beach was a welcome sight for all of us, coming from red desert to white sand and a tropical town. Then we called into more family members in Sydney, cousin Tracey's parents, dropping her off before we drove back to Melbourne.

I felt so lucky to have been on such a great adventure instead of being put in respite foster care, which often happens to foster kids when their foster families go on holidays. Family was a new concept to me. Apart from my short time with Aunty Kerry and Uncle Theo, I had never had a formal family structure before.

# CHAPTER 11

# WHERE DO I FIT IN?

When Rey recovered and was discharged home from the hospital, Joan would arrange access for me to see him. My visits with him always left me disappointed. He would still turn up late or cancel last minute. When he did turn up, and I would stay the weekend with him, we never had any father-son time.

He would take me to his friends' parties and proudly introduce me to his friends, saying "This is my son!" Then they would sit around and talk in Tagalog, the Filipino language that I didn't understand or speak. Today, I see my mates with their kids, and they seem to have made a conscious effort to connect and spend quality time with their kids; perhaps because our generation all had either absent or shitty fathers.

I don't know why I bothered to continue going to Rey's for visits. I don't understand why he wanted to have me over for the weekend, he never spent any time with me. Was it so he could put a front on for his friends to show them that he was trying to be a good father? Maybe he was trying in his own way, I don't know. I kept hoping that maybe, eventually, we might bond. But it never happened, and I just kept wasting my time and kept opening myself up for constant disappointment to point I would come back home to the Grahams angry. What a waste of time.

I kept asking about my mother, but no one knew where she was living. Joan would get frustrated with me because she would try to get me to open up about my feelings. I did want to express them, but every time I tried, I would feel an overwhelming sense of anxiety, and I couldn't speak.

When I would lay in my bed of a night, I would often cry myself to sleep releasing the angst that had built up inside, and the pain of the rejection I felt from my father and mother. At times I just wanted my Mum, to hear it from her own mouth and not from others that she didn't want me. Instead, I was stuck with my father, who I just couldn't work out. Why did he want to continue to see me? On his visitation weekends, he never spends any time with me or never showed a real interest in me.

*28/9/1988 Home Visit to Joan Graham's with Rey*
*Shane was pleased to see Rey, but Rey was pretty uninterested in Shane. Rey asked to leave after 25 minutes. Rey did not open*

*Shane's Father's Day present – "I'll open it up when I get home"
Rey said. Rey was also unwilling to go outside with Shane and
look at the horses, "Next time I'll go" Rey said.*

*One the drive back to Rey's I went over the review with Rey,
particularly the access. It is obviously challenging for him to
understand Shane's needs when he has never had much to do with
him. Rey was more concerned to know whether Shane would be
able to choose where he wants to live when he gets older.*

*We discussed the possibility of Shane residing in foster care
permanently until he reaches 17 years old. Rey seemed satisfied
with this, although it is hard to know what he is really feeling. He
agreed to come to the review. I will collect him Monday morning.*
**Sarah Jackson – Social Worker.**

### 03/10/1988 Placement review meeting

*Jannette, the Department of Health Services worker, said that a
'permanent foster care application' should be considered over the
next 6 months for Shane and the Grahams.*

*Joan said she feels that Shane is a difficult child to get close
to and 'love.' Joan thinks that he still has difficulty being straight
with her about how he is feeling and is still feeling his way with
her. She agrees that he seems to relate better and more easily and
that Brian, Paul and Scott have no trouble in accepting him as a
permanent member of the family.*

*Another meeting will be called in 6 months to consider perma-
nent placement. The Grahams will need this time to reach a decision.* **Sarah Jackson – Social Worker.**

Joan was unsure whether the placement was going to be bene-
ficial for me and for her and the rest of the family. Joan always

wanted to do the best for the children under her care as well as getting fulfilment back in return. Reading my foster care file and seeing these struggles Joan had with me as a child, I begin to wonder if the placement was right for anyone at that time. If this didn't work out, and there was no other family to take me, then I would have ended up in Allambie, the house for unwanted boys.

Rey wasn't too interested in what happened to me, it was like he just gave up fighting for me. Did he even start? It seemed that the only people in my life that were in my corner were the Graham's who I had only known for two years.

The thing I now know of depression is the apathy one has with this illness. As a ten-year-old boy with a new family and environment, I should have been a happy child - I had good and bad days. Back in the '80s and 90's mental illness was hardly talked about, especially in children and adolescents.

The assessments are written by my social workers always said, 'no apparent psychological issues', but were they blind or did they not have the skills in mental health assessment to recognise my mental health issues? Maybe the latter. Even though I was with a stable, kind, caring foster family, as a foster kid you have that feeling in the pit of your stomach that this is temporary; *don't get too comfortable because you could be on the move again.* I had already had four other past homes from the age of two – my mother and father when they were married, my grandparents, my aunt and uncle, and my father, making the Graham's my fifth home.

I wanted so desperately to fit into the Graham family. To be like Paul and Scott who were interested in boy things like cars and motorbikes, playing football, have a lot of guy friends, like in the football club. But I was so shit at team sports that football never lasted long, and it was too rough of a game for me.

I wanted to be more open with my feelings with Joan, but I couldn't trust that if told her my deepest darkest secret that she wouldn't send me packing. I thought Brian, Paul and Scott would hate me, and I would be all alone again. But harbouring this secret didn't do me any good either, and my interests in dancing, singing and acting didn't align with the rest of the family's.

I know Joan was trying to do the best she could do to help me fit in with other boys my age, like enrolling me into scouts, football and encouraging me to play with more boys at school than the girls. But what she didn't know, and something I couldn't tell her but desperately wanted to release this secret that had been clamming me up for so long.

*I think that I am gay.*

I struggled with this as I didn't want to be gay, I wanted to be normal. One night around the dinner table, the topic of homosexuality came up. Joan would say that it was unnatural, and she didn't understand why people would choose to live that life. Paul and Scott would agree. Paul, the one person I looked up to, would start teasing me about being gay because I liked girls activities. Brian would shut them down, saying "That's enough!", Using his stern voice. The boys would stop teasing me, and I would sit there quietly trying to finish my dinner without crying. If only they knew the truth, I thought. They weren't bigoted people as the family were very much involved in community charities and accepting of all. It didn't matter where you came from. I think that back in those times, homosexuality wasn't accepted or understood as much as it is today. They had never known a gay person, they lived in a mainly Caucasian, country old suburban town. I kept quiet and struggled silently. I always wondered if I had just opened up and wasn't afraid of telling my truth if things would have ended up differently.

# CHAPTER 12

# FAMILIES

As a forty-year-old man, sometimes I feel like a child trapped in a man's body. Research into the developmental issues of children being in foster care suggests that children in their early developmental years who have come from neglect or family violence have some psychological and developmental problems, often affecting them through adolescence and adulthood. The psychological impacts consist of detachment issues, developmental delays, mental health issues such as depression and anxiety in the context of the ability to cope with stress, environmental and social factors.

During adolescence, these childhood issues can manifest into areas where the adolescent becomes withdrawn, isolative, defiant and displays antisocial behaviours. As I was entering my teenage years, Joan and Brian would get frustrated with my actions and lack of thought of anyone else but myself. As a family, they were involved in community activities and had the values of helping others before themselves, and our personalities seemed poles apart. They were extroverted, and I was more introverted.

I was different, and although the Graham's tried their best to help me feel like I belonged, there was a part of me that felt like I didn't belong anywhere. In my foster care file, Joan would say that I was self-centred and hard to get close to and love. Sarah, my new social worker, gave them information about detachment disorder. I found it hard to form bonds with people due to the trauma and neglect I had endured as a young child. Over time Joan and my relationship improved, and I slowly became more outgoing, but I was always emotionally half empty on the inside.

When I went into care, my Aunt and Uncle had no idea where I was placed. Uncle Theo said he was looking for me for months. Oz Child had moved offices from the old double story white house to another location in Dandenong. In their search for me, they went to the old white house and realised that the agency had moved –they just didn't know where. It had been a few years since I last saw them. Actually, I never saw them after Rey took me. As a kid, I always wondered when I became a state ward, why didn't they rescue me and take me back. Why didn't any of my family want me? Where was my sister Christine?

**Shane's contact with Wakefield family update 27th of February 1989**

*Shane saw the Wakefield's briefly in April 1988 at Fountain Gate Shopping Centre. They then rang Joan to ask if they could take him away for the weekend. Joan ask them to ring the agency since that weekend was not possible. Joan said the agency could arrange for another weekend with her and to make sure it was possible for him to go. I spoke to Theo in May, and he said he would talk with Kerry about another day and then get back to me- he never did. Shane met up with his cousin Tania at a young creative writer's day in November. In January, Kerry and Theo contacted the agency regarding seeing Shane and giving him some Christmas presents.*

*They seem to have been some misunderstanding about the contact arrangements for seeing Shane last May - they had felt that since Shane had lived with them for one year, they should be able to take him for a whole weekend rather than just for the day initially, as suggested, and could not accept having to go through the agency. However, after an initial visit to the Graham's with Kerry, Tania and Leonie on the 17th January 1989, Shane spent the day with the Wakefield's on 18th January 1989. With a home visit by myself to discuss with Kerry and Theo Shane's future on 8th of February 1989, the Wakefield's decided they would like to remain in contact with Shane on a more regular basis.*

*Shane then spent a weekend with them at their holiday home in Walkerville on 18th and 19th of February 1989. He seemed to really enjoy himself, especially as Christine (his half-sister) was there too with her little boy Lee (four years old) and according to the Wakefield's he was no trouble at all. I arranged with Kerry to contact Joan directly for further visits then Joan notifies the agency. Shane then spent another weekend with the Wakefield's on the 15th and 16th of April 1989.*

*After the first visit with the Wakefield's, Shane wanted to know why he couldn't go back and live with them again. Tania and Leonie had asked him to stay and live with them again. I explained that it was not up to Tania and Leonie, but Kerry and Theo's decision and that although they would like to see Shane regularly, they were not able to have another child in the home. Shane did seem to accept this. We then discussed him remaining with the Graham's and how much he felt a member of the family. He was reluctant in answering but eventually said he would like to stay with the Graham's.*

*I discussed with Kerry the effect that Tania and Leonie had by asking Shane to live with them, and Kerry said she was aware that had happened, and she had explained to the girls that it was not possible and ask them to not mention it to Shane again.* **Sarah Jackson – Social Worker.**


At that time, I liked being with the Grahams'. They were friendly people, but there is nothing like being with family – blood relations. Aunty Kerry and Uncle Theo's excuse was that they couldn't afford to have me live with them, even though they would receive tax-free carers benefits to assist them with clothes and schooling. My sister's life was chaotic as she struggled to bring up her son Lee at 20 years old. After being reunited with my extended family, I would spend school holidays, weekends and time over the Christmas break with my aunt, my uncle and cousins Tania and Leonie, up at their Walkerville beach house. During the festive season, they would shower me with gifts and Joan became concerned that I would start to expect that from my family every time I saw them, and this was sending the wrong message. Maybe overcompensating by giving me material things eased the burden of their guilt for leaving me in foster care. I did love and enjoy being with my family and my cousins.

The only times I saw my extended family was when they went away or at birthday parties, which I would get an invite at the last minute, like an afterthought I would get a phone call on the same day. This would upset Joan as she would have to drop everything to arrange transportation to get me there.

I always enjoyed seeing my family. I started having weekend access with Christine and seeing my nephew, Lee. Upon returning home after seeing my family, I would get depressed as I longed to live with my family. I never expressed my feelings to Joan as I didn't want to upset or hurt anyone's feelings. Instead, I pushed them down deep inside and pretended that everything was fine, but I wasn't okay.

# CHAPTER 13

# POWERLESS

Every child matures to a point where they see their parents as adults, not just as their parents but as people. Joan would tell me that she wasn't my mother, nor would she try to be. However, she was my guardian, and my mother figure and Brian was my father figure. They would be there for me during the good and the bad, and all I had to do was trust that. I know that they loved me like their own children, and I didn't want for anything. So, I don't understand why my behaviour became so challenging as I was entering my adolescent years. Reading my foster care file, Joan would say I could be self-centred at times, that I lacked common sense, and my values were polar apart from the rest of the family.

There was always a void, an emptiness I felt, and even though I had a family that cared about me, there's nothing that can compare to blood. I have questions to try and understand my biological makeup and personality, my mental health problems, and why I acted the way I did. People tell me I look like my Dad, but I have traits of Mum's personality. I remember a time when I was visiting Aunty Kerry and Uncle Theo, and we were talking about what qualities we have gotten from our parents, and Aunty Kerry said, 'You have your Mum's selfish side.' A bit harsh, I thought, since I didn't get the chance to know what my Mum was like, but thanks for that.

No one in my family can explain why Mum went off the rails and rebelled at fifteen. Was it that due to Mum's severe epilepsy that leads to frontal lobe damage, that impaired her thinking, reasoning or impacted on her personality? Questions that now I will never get answers to. When I was in care, no one knew where she was living. I desperately wanted to see her, especially now that I am older, I wanted to know who my mum was. My family tried to protect me from her impulsiveness and avoid me from getting hurt. However, I felt that was my decision to make, my risk to take and looking back, I feel robbed of that opportunity. I was twelve years old turning thirteen, and I think I was old enough to make that choice.

The adults in my life also decided to choose, when Pop had a heart attack and ended up in the hospital, not to tell me, and again I felt robbed of the chance to say good-bye to him. I remember the day Uncle Theo phoned me to tell me the news. I was sitting out the back sheds watching Paul work on his car. When Joan yelled out to tell me my uncle was on the phone I raced up the path to the house, excited to hear from him. After I heard the news, I was in shock and didn't say much and passed the phone back to Joan. I walked back down to the sheds where

Paul was and quietly sat down against the wall staring blankly into space. Joan walked down and sat next to me and said,

"Are you OK mate?" I looked at her and burst into tears. She hugged me while I cried on her shoulder.

'What"s happened?" Paul asked, concerned.

"His grandfather passed away" she answered.

"Oh shit, I'm so sorry mate" Paul said.


### Home Visit to Theo and Kerry 8th February 1989

*When I visited Theo and Kerry on 8th of February 1989, they told me that Charlie Wakefield was in Monash medical centre recovering from a heart attack and hemorrhage from the bowel. He had been staying with Christine when he moved from Phillip Island to Sandringham when it happened. Theo and Christine were wondering whether they should tell Shane about his Grandfather, but we all agreed that it would be better for Shane to see Charlie once he was out of the hospital which seems likely at the time. However, sadly, Charlie died suddenly four days later.*

*Shane did not attend the funeral since Tania and Leonie we're not going, and Joan did not feel it was appropriate especially as so much had happened to Shane over the last few months - seeing Rey again, reconnecting with the Wakefield's, school camp etc.*

*Kerry and Theo and took Shane around to Charlie's house in Phillip Island on the way back from Walkerville and Shane was able to take some of Charlie's things as keepsakes. Kerry and Theo managed to contact Bernice after not having heard from her for 4 years, about Charlie's death and whether she would come to the funeral. Bernice was very hostile and accused them of taking Shane away from her. She was not sure whether she would come to the funeral or not. Bernice is now living in Noble Park with her partner Brian.*

*Kerry and Theo are worried about Bernice suddenly turning up in Shane's life again. They have spoken with Christine about it too, and everyone agrees that Shane should be given more time to settle with the Graham's before any contact with Bernice should be made. Shane has been asking about how to find Bernice for some time however nobody seemed to know her whereabouts until now.*

*While I sense Joan and Kerry are concerned about tracing Bernice and Shane getting hurt, I tend not to share their level of concern. Shane seems to view this situation quite realistically and does not appear to hold any unrealistic expectations. I told Shane I had spoken to Kerry about contacting Bernice and he was keen to hear any information she had. I was honest with Shane and said that Kerry and Theo felt Bernice was too self- centred.*

*Shane also asks me what would happen to him if he was not placed with the Grahams. I explained that he probably would have gone to Allambie an orphanage for children that were wards of the state.* **Sarah Jackson, Social Worker**


Sarah noticed my maturity and realistic views I had towards my mother. I knew she was unreliable; I didn't have any romantic ideas that she should see me and want me back in her life again and want to be my mother. I understood the need for my family to want to protect me from any further trauma, but I don't believe this was the right decision on their behalf.

I should have been able to make my own decisions as to whether I wanted to see my mother, see my pop in the hospital or attend his funeral when he died. I don't hold any resentment towards my family; however, I can't describe the feeling of being cheated. Pop died all alone in the hospital, and that took me a long time to get over.

I was never told that Bernice lived in Noble Park or that she had a partner named Brian. I was told no one knew where she was living, but when I turned eighteen and got a copy of my foster care file, I found out the truth. My mother's address was 38 Heighington Street Noble Park Victoria, and ironically, she only lived twenty minutes from my foster family's farm in Hampton Park, both suburbs in the south-eastern region of Victoria. When I first learnt of this, I felt angered and betReyed. How could she live only twenty minutes away and I never got to see her?

I just wished that I was given a bit more credit. I didn't need protecting. I needed to know where I came from. I wanted to know my mother, regardless of the outcome. If she hurt me by rejecting me then so be it, but at least I could have had the opportunity to confront her face to face and ask the question "Why don't you want me?" Even if the truth hurt at least I would have had closure, or if she wanted me in her life and I started having access with her and was left disappointed that it was better than not knowing at all.

I was already disappointed continuously by my father, but he was still able to see me if I wanted to see him, so I can't understand why the same situation wasn't extended to my mother. Hurt cannot be healed without knowing the answers as to why you're hurting in the first place. Like I said, I wish I was given more credit as a ten-year-old to make my own decision to see my mother and not have the decision made for me.

# CHAPTER 14

# LIFE CHANGES & GROWING UP

Throughout my time in foster care, I had social workers come and go from my life. Not the best thing for a kid with abandonment and attachment issues. I would get used to one worker who you slowly trusted and formed a bond with and then they would move on. I now understand people don't stay in services for long periods as the desire for professional development and new challenges arise; but already at a young age, I was aware that no one sticks around in my life for long.

Sarah had left, and I had been introduced to a new worker named Jacob. Jacob looked young for his age. He had one of those baby faces and looked like this was his first job, fresh out of University. Jacob was a tall Caucasian guy with a slim build and short, brown, wavy hair. Jacob appeared to be the reserved type, but from what I can remember, he was fun to be around.

I bonded easily to Jacob. He was the first male social worker I had, all the others were female, and it was nice to have another male influence. My foster dad Brian would tell him jokes that would make him blush, probably to get Jacob to come out of his shell a bit more.

### 10/05/1989: Home Visit to Grahams

*It was an excellent opportunity to establish rapport with Shane. Last time when I visited with Sarah, we gave Shane a folder to put some family photos in, which he'd done by this evening. I, therefore, thought it would be good to go through Shane's family tree with him, so he could put that in with his photos.*

*Shane enjoyed this. He was most surprised to find out that Bernice had two children that had been adopted out. Shane hadn't known that before. He is going to ask Christine (preferred to be called Chris) about them next time he sees her. **Jacob Conner – Social Worker.***

When I asked my sister Chris, she confirmed what I had found out from my previous visit from Jacob. I was shocked and puzzled why no one in the family ever told me. "How do we find them?" I asked her. Chris said she had been trying but had been unsuccessful thus far. She did tell me that we had a brother and a sister that mum had adopted out and that their names were Douglas and Julie. Chris and Douglas had the same father and Julie had a German father. That's why there is ten years difference between Chris and I. Apparently, it costs a lot of money to search for adoptive children and at this time in Chris's life she couldn't afford to. "Maybe we can try and find them down the track when I can afford to" Chris said. We had worked out that our brother Douglas was two years younger than Chris and nine years older than me. Our sister Julie was five years older than me and six years younger than Chris and four years younger than Douglas.

Discovering this new family information, I would imagine what it would have been like having had lived with all my siblings. How our lives would have been different. I would wonder what lives my adopted-out siblings would have had. Were they happy? What were their adoptive families like? Did they know about Chris and me? Questions I would never know the answers to until I was old enough to search for them myself. I had always felt a great deal of pain. Knowing your mother didn't want you, and the rejection would cause problems for me with future relationships. But learning that I had two siblings out in the world somewhere, made me realise that my mother didn't just abandon me, she left all four of us! What type of person could carry each of us for nine months, give birth to us then leave us? No wonder Chris didn't want anything to do with her.

I was in Grade Six, the final year of primary school, and I had a normal childhood. I would only see Rey occasionally, and I would see my extended family and my sister Chris on school holidays and some weekends when we went up to the beach house in Walkerville. My behaviour was beginning to frustrate Joan and Brian, and I was being told I was taking Joan for granted by expecting things to be done for me. I guess it was a part of fitting in with the family and pitching in with chores around the house, but sometimes I would neglect my chores, and Joan would just find it easier to do them herself.

**05/09/1989: *Home visit Grahams.***

*I intended to discuss with Shane the need for him to take more responsibility in the household and not take Joan (in particular) for granted. Instead, we again discussed family trees. Shane was very interested in constructing his own family tree and had a look at Joan's family history to get an idea about how it is done. I said I would send him whatever relevant information was on file to fill in the gaps. Shane was also interested in seeing his grandfather's headstone (Charlie Wakefield). I will ring the Crematorium to see whether it's in place and if so, either Joan or myself will take him to have a look.*

*Shane seems to have a natural and genuine curiosity to find out more about his family. It seems as if he is trying to put together the pieces of a very complex puzzle.* **Jacob Conner – Social Worker.**

As I was getting older, I attempted to not take Joan for granted and be more responsible in taking care of my pet birds, feeding the dogs, helping around the farm etc. I had finished Grade Six and was about to start high school the following year. I would spend Christmas between my dad's, my Aunt and Uncle's beach house in Walkerville and Loch Sport, water skiing with Paul and Scott and other cousins on Brian's side of the family. Jacob mentioned that he noticed that I took direction from my older foster brother Paul who was twenty at the time. When I was thirteen, I thought I could go everywhere Paul and Scott went, but Joan would have to put a dampener on my plans, so Paul and Scott didn't have to look after me all the time. If I'm honest, I would get pissed off when I couldn't go shooting or motorbike riding with them.

Jacob was only my worker for about a year before leaving the foster care agency, and I was introduced to a new worker Sally Connor. Saying goodbye to Jacob was hard as I bonded with him the most out of the other workers. Sally was in her mid-twenties, and when I went through my horrible adolescent years, I don't think she handled my situation quite right. Even though I now know that she would have tried her best, things could have been handled differently, maybe there was a lack of education in mental health in the early 90s. Perhaps it was due to her lack of experience that I didn't get the psychological help I really needed.

# CHAPTER 15

# HIGH SCHOOL BULLYING

It was the summer of 1992; I had just completed Year Seven and was going into Year Eight. Over the school holidays, my best friend Justin would come over to hang out. Justin was about to go into Year Nine, and even though he was a year older than me, I was happy that we hadn't had drifted apart in high school. Our farm was a fifteen minutes bike ride from Justin's house. We were best friends in primary school and in a Grade Five-Six composite class when we met. When we made it to high school, Justin was in Year Eight, and I was in Year Seven at the time. I had my best friend back! We hung around with each other at lunchtimes during my first year at school. That year we performed in the high school musical in which we played a pair of half-witted safari explorers. Together we got the audience laughing.

On the summer school break, we would go to each other's houses. Justin used to ride his bike over to the farm, and we would play out in the back sheds. On one of the weekends when he was over, we were hanging out in one of the little sheds off the main hay shed. As teenage boys do, we thought it was funny to compare dick sizes to see who had the biggest. So, we pulled out our dicks to compare sizes. They were pretty much the same size.

"Wonder who's got the biggest stiffies?" Justin asked.

We wrapped our hands around each other's and started to pull each other. As they both swelled up, we measured again, putting them side by side.

"I win!" Justin said proudly.

We started to rub against each other. I was shaking. My heart was beating fast as I couldn't believe this was happening. Justin started to pull me, and I followed suit and did the same to him until we both ejaculated in each other's hands. We quickly pulled up our pants and went to the tap and washed the semen off our hands. Justin seemed freaked out and picked up his bike. "I've gotta go!" He rode his bike so fast up our long driveway. Lucky the front gate was open, so he didn't have to stop- a swift getaway. I felt a bit confused and saddened that Justin left so suddenly. I never heard from him much after that day. When I called him to ask if he wanted to hang out, Justin would say he was busy, or he had family stuff on. I tried to talk to him about what we did, but he would shut me down or change the subject.

For the rest of the summer I never saw him as I would go away with foster siblings Michelle and her husband Greg, Leanne and her husband Mark, Paul and Scott, to the beach house in Loch Sport. The girls would have fun being pulled along behind the boat sitting in the blow-up doughnut, laughing as they skimmed across the water of the lake. My brother-in-law and Scott would kneeboard. I was envious as I wasn't great at knee boarding as I didn't have the upper body strength to pull myself back onto the board when I fell off.

Year Nine is known as the year that teenagers can be at their worst. With hormones raging in their bodies, bad attitudes and the popular kids being horrible to the unpopular kids, Year Nine is the worst. It became hell for me. I hadn't seen Justin for four weeks since our last hang out. Towards the end of lunch, I saw him at the boy's locker bay. He had a new haircut and looked good. I walked over to him, feeling a little nervous.

"Hey Just, how you been?" I asked.

"Fine" Justin said, looking straight ahead and not making eye contact with me, his demeanour cold. We stood there in awkward silence. Standing next to his locker, I watched him get his books for class.

"So, Year Ten 'aye? Moving up in the world" I joked.

"Listen, I don't think we should hang out anymore," Justin said, still not looking at me.

"Why," I asked.

"Cos I'm not a poof OK!" Justin snapped. He slammed his locker shut and shoved me with his shoulder as he walked past. I walked fast to the toilets making sure no one was in there and went into one of the cubicles, locked the door, sat on the toilet seat and allowed myself to cry. The next day at school, he started calling me a poof in front of his Year Ten mates as they walked past me laughing. I was shocked and hurt that my best friend had turned against me. That's when the bullying started for me. Justin told people that I confessed to giving guys blow jobs and like Chinese whispers, this rumour had circulated around the school with made up extras added onto it. *'Being a foster kid, I had to suck guys off for money!'*

The popular kids started calling me *'Hoover'*, making vacuum sounds as I walked past in the corridor. This went on for all of Year Eight and Year Nine. I lost friends and school life for me began to be hell on earth. I guess Justin got in first so if I made a claim that it was Justin who instigated our encounter no one would believe me. He was popular, and now, I was not. Before I knew it, I was ostracised by the popular group of friends I'd had the last year. The rumours trickled down to my year level, and I began to be tormented by some of the other Year Nine kids. I didn't have any friends and found myself walking around school on my own or hiding in the library during lunchtime.

I hated our physical education (P.E) class; I was not good at footy or cricket, and the sporty boys would call me a *"dickhead"* or a *"stupid poof"* when I dropped the ball. In the change rooms, they would ridicule me shouting out *"Look out boys, stand against the wall Shane's here!"* The jock boys would laugh. After enduring weeks of constant bullying, I snapped and told them all to "FUCK OFF!" Billy the ringleader shoves me up against the wall with his hand around my neck. I couldn't breathe. I tried to get my fingers underneath his hand to loosen his grip, but he was stronger than me. I refused to show fear or weakness and just glared into his eyes.

"What did you say fag?"

After a few seconds, he let me go and pushed me on the floor. Billy and his mates walked past laughing as I gasped for air holding my throat. I wished that Scott was still at school. He had finished Year Twelve last year. When I had started Year Seven in high school, I had a problem with a group of boys teasing me. When I told Scott, he gathered some of his mates and pushed these boys around while they played basketball at lunch, warning them off me. I never had any more problems with them for the rest of the year. Now with Scott gone, I had no one to look out for me - I was all alone.

I started to not bring my sports uniform to school on the days we had P.E, so I didn't have to go into the change room or play sport with those arseholes. Mr Brown, our P.E teacher, would give me warnings. Sometimes I would write notes forging Joan's signature with some excuse as to why I couldn't participate in sport. I would go to the library instead and work on an assignment coming up. The library started to become my sanctuary but also where I isolated myself whenever I could so I could get away from their daily torment.

I started hanging out with a group of misfit girls in the year above. Jules would tell me not to worry about those dickheads. We would hang around the back of the oval with the seniors. Everyone who smoked would hang around the end of the oval at lunchtime as the large gum trees provided hiding spots from the teacher's view. The teachers had no chance of catching anyone out as you had a full view of the oval and could warn each other if a teacher was spotted. To fit in, I started to smoke. I was happy I had some friends and that my isolation in the library had come to an end. But that didn't stop the bullies in my year level tormenting me.

Home life wasn't too good for me either. I would get into fights with Joan as she grew frustrated with my behaviour, and

I became isolative and withdrawn. Joan would try and get me to open about my feelings, but I would just get anxious and couldn't talk, minimising the troubles I had at school. I was so different from the rest of the family and felt I didn't fit in. I had difficulty accepting I was gay and fearful of my foster family, rejecting me. I kept that side of me a secret. I developed a bad attitude at school and started getting detentions for being a smart arse to teachers. The bullying started to slow down as the jocks got bored of me and moved onto someone else. Justin never spoke to me again, and I just felt alone. I was only thirteen, and I started to think about what it would be like to kill myself. My new social worker Sally would come over for home visits to see how I was going and then privately talk with Joan.

**4th of March 1992 home visit to Shane and the Graham's**
*Joan mentioned that Shane had received further detention and has been threatened with suspension - again being disrespectful towards teachers. Shane is easily led and is probably heading for a stormy adolescence.*

*We briefly discussed my concern that Shane may eventually shoot through and not maintain any contact despite all the time the Graham's have put in with him. Joan admitted that she also shared my concern. I suggested to Joan that Shane's early experiences and his nature seem to make a difficult for Shane to develop close relationships due to his detachment disorder.*

*I feel that Joan senses that Shane does not belong with the Grahams. Their fundamental values are poles apart - Shane tends to be self-centred, whereas the Graham's highly value sharing and giving help to others. Shane is introverted, and the Graham's are an outgoing family. He does not fit culturally with the family nor does he like boys activities, for example, sports like the Graham's sons. Unfortunately, the match between Shane and the Grahams is not good; that's why I believe the placement stands a very good chance of failing in the next couple of years.* **Sally Conway – Social Worker**

**7th of May 1992: Home visit to Joan and Brian Graham.**
*Joan admitted the placement can be frustrating there as Shane doesn't fit into the Graham family. Joan said she wished that Shane could fit in and keep his own personality, but unfortunately this will never happen. Joan and I discussed the fact that Shane really has no place where 'he fits in', he doesn't fit in with the Wakefield's Danish and English, the Grahams are Australian, and his father's Filipino and Shane doesn't know how to speak the language. Shane doesn't have a culture he can really relate to.*

*In discussing Shane's placement in our weekly case meetings, I provided an update of Shane's arrangement. I suggested that adolescence may be a rocky period for Shane and the Grahams* **Sally Conway – Social Worker**

# CHAPTER 16

# STORMY ADOLESCENCE

*I hear a voice call out my name. 'Shane it's time for lunch' That sounds vaguely familiar. I turn around, and I see Nan standing at the back door, wearing her apron as she always did when she cook the traditional Sunday roast. I run towards her. Leap into her arms as she hugs me. Nan's hugs always made you feel like everything was alright. "Wash your hands you silly sausage" Nan would say laughing. I go into the bathroom to wash my hands. I'm five years old and can't reach the taps, but Nan's behind me to help me. As I dry my hands on the hand towel, I can hear laughing and chatter coming from the kitchen.*

*As I walk into the kitchen, I see the whole family sitting around the dining table. Mum,*

*Dad, Christine, Uncle Theo, Aunty Kerry, Pop, my cousins Tania, Leonie and Shez waiting for me. The table is covered with food. Roast beef and chicken, roasted potatoes, pumpkin and a bowl of peas. I sat on mum's lap. She had already fixed me a plate and cut up the meat for me. Mum kisses me on my head, "I love you, my sweet boy" she says as she helps me eat my food.*

*I'm happy. Content. I'm with my family...*

I suddenly wake up to the darkness. I look over to my alarm clock, its 3am in the morning. Was that a vivid memory or just a dream? I couldn't tell you. I wished it was a memory. I felt cheated! I closed my eyes desperately willing my brain to take me back. Nothing. I'm overcome with sadness when I realise, I'm alone. Tears stream down my face as I turn over to face the wall. I close my eyes and fall back to sleep.

Sally was right when she thought that adolescence would be a rocky period between the Grahams and me. Things had been bubbling away under the surface: I was being bullied at school, I had no friends, I was angry at Rey for never spending time with me when I would go to see him on weekends, and I knew I was gay but too scared to come out in fear of being rejected by the family. I never said anything, and I just kept it all inside until one day, the littlest thing made me explode.

### 01/03/1993: Phone Call from Shane

*Shane says he wants to move on- doesn't want to live with the Grahams any longer. Shane asked if he could live with the Wakefield's, Christine or Ambelle.*

*Spoke to Joan. Joan said that a few recent incidents had occurred (e.g. Shane borrowing a coat and not treating it correctly) and Shane had been furious this morning when he was not allowed to do as he wanted.*

*Arranged to visit Shane that afternoon.* **Sally Conway – Social Worker**


### 01/03/1993: Home Visit to Shane.

*Shane feeling unsupported by the Grahams in his interests, acting, singing, dancing – said Paul gives him a hard time. Said he felt restricted in what he could and couldn't do. He thought that even when he tried to make an effort regarding completing chores around the house, it was never good enough. Shane thought that the age difference between himself and the Graham boys was very noticeable and a problem. He also mentioned not feeling close to any member of his foster family.*

*Shane would like to live with his Aunt and Uncle (the Wakefield's) – Likes Tania and Leonie's company. Also, Shane suggested he might be able to live with Christine, her fiancé Mark and his nephew Lee or his other sister Ambelle and her husband Shane if the Wakefield's weren't an option. I told Shane that I would contact his Aunt and Uncle.* **Sally Conway – Social Worker**


### 01/03/1993: Visit Joan (at the Oz Child op Shop)

*Joan volunteers at the op shop every Monday. Joan feeling very flat and disappointed. Feels she has done all she can for Shane and that if he wants to leave, then it would be better for everyone if he did. Joan admitted feeling quite frustrated with the placement over the years as she felt she couldn't get anywhere' with Shane. Joan concerned about Brian's health and her own health of stress of placement continues.* **Sally Conway – Social Worker**

### 02/03/1993: Phone call from Theo Wakefield

*Theo appeared to feel some responsibility to Shane but raised many problems with taking him.*

1. *Pressure it would put on the family, Kerry and Leonie not keen.*
2. *Leonie and Shane clashed last time they lived together.*
3. *Shane would put financial pressure on the family.*

*Theo has spoken to Christine, and they are getting together tonight to discuss if they feel they can offer Shane a placement. I suggested that if they were not really sure they could meet Shane's needs that it would be better to continue with holiday placements than jeopardise a breakdown which would destroy relationships.* **Sally Conway – Social Worker**

### 02/03/1993: Phone call from Christine Wakefield.

*Christine feels she lacked the money, time and space for Shane at present. Christine impressed as having a good understanding of Shane's needs and personality/values. She seemed quite concerned about his future, asking about the options for him. I also tried to tell Christine (as I did Theo) that I did not want her to feel pressure to take Shane.* **Sally Conway – Social Worker**

**09/03/1993: *Phone call from Theo Wakefield.***

*The Wakefield's decided that they are not able to take Shane – will discuss further tonight.*

**09/03/1993: Home visit to the Wakefield's with Shane. Christine and Mark also present.**

*Theo outlined reasons for not being able to take Shane:*

1.  *Problems between their own marriage.*
2.  *Kerry's Illness (Lupus)*
3.  *Financial Stresses*
4.  *Concerns about Shane getting along with Tania and Leonie.*
5.  *Concerns about Shane fitting in re: Theo's discipline and strict rules.*

*All present felt Shane was going through a teenage stage and could not comprehend how he could not feel a part of the Graham family after nearly 6 years. I talked about the changes Shane had experienced and the difficulty that he presents in forming attachments and having a sense of belonging. I also discussed Shane's desire to be with his biological family. The family thought it would be best for Shane to stay with the Grahams and to spend holidays with them. Shane very close to tears on a few occasions.*

*On the journey home, Shane said he wasn't disappointed, but his body language suggested he was quite upset. Shane said that he would be giving up a lot by leaving the Grahams and perhaps he should stay. I suggested to Shane he gives serious thought to what he wants to do over the next couple of days and that the Grahams were very upset and staying may not be an option.*

*I gave Joan and Brian information on Detachment Disorder to help make sense of his behaviour.* **Sally Conway – Social Worker**

When Sally was driving me to my Aunt and Uncles for the family meeting, nothing was said to me about everyone's decision not to have me live with them. I wish Sally told me because I was hopeful, hopeful that the answer would be yes and that I would be able to live with my family. I felt blindsided as I was sat on a dining chair in the middle of the lounge room facing everyone sitting on my Aunt and Uncle's long u-shaped sofa, listening to the excuses as to why no one wanted me. To the adults, their reasons seemed logical and practical, but to a fourteen-year-old teenager, desperate to be with his family, all I heard was why I wasn't worthy or good enough for them to have me. Writing this chapter brings tears to my eyes as I relive the rejection, I felt from my family that night. I felt like I had no one, and I was all alone. At this moment, I wished I was dead or never had been born, then I wouldn't be a burden, an unwanted child that no one knew what to do with. I didn't hear from my family for a while after that 'family' meeting. Joan was disappointed with the Wakefield's that they went away to Walkerville for the Easter break and I didn't get an invitation despite them knowing my placement was 'shaky' and that Joan and the family would have welcomed the break.

In the weeks that followed, I tried to make a conscious effort to help around the house, do my chores, apologise to the Graham's for my behaviour, but the damage had been done. That one phone call I made to Sally when I was angry, saying I wanted to move I had single headedly blown up my life.

*14/04/1993: Phone Call to Joan.*

*Joan has come to the point to end the placement and Shane should move on. She feels it would be better to maintain a relationship with Shane via weekends, holidays etc. than jeopardise a complete placement breakdown with ill feelings on all sides.* **Sally Conway – Social Worker**

And that was it. I started something that couldn't be undone. In bed, I would cry into my pillow so no one could hear. I felt totally alone. I felt that Brian and the boys hated me because they wouldn't speak to me much. I thought about killing myself a lot. I just had to think about the least painful way. I needed a release of my pain, so one night, when I was having a bath, I cut my inner thigh with a small kitchen knife. I could feel a sudden release as I watched the blood trickle down my leg into the bath water turning the water pink. I moved the blade onto my wrists. I wanted to cut the veins I could see through my skin but chickened out. I could hear my voice in my head telling me how worthless I was, that my family didn't want me because I was ugly and a loser, a selfish cunt, a nobody, and if I had died at birth then I wouldn't be anybody's problem. I couldn't escape my own voice in my head. I kept quiet and didn't tell anyone. I thought maybe I deserved this torture. Suicidal thoughts were always in my head, and then I heard of a guy at school that tried to hang himself, but he survived. *If I decided to hang myself, then I would make sure I was dead,* I thought.

# CHAPTER 17

# GOODBYE WORLD

I felt like I had no way out. I was gay, I didn't fit in anywhere, and my own maternal family didn't want me. In the past, the boys would tease me about being gay because of my interests in theatre and horses. Unbeknownst to them, I was, but I was fearful of rejection if I came out to them, so I never said anything. I was ashamed and hated myself for being so unnatural, a sin – *why couldn't I have been born straight?*

The weekend after my meeting with my family, I felt rejected, lost and worthless. I was in my darkest place and the lowest I have ever been to. *No one wants me! I don't fit in anywhere, I'm gay, why couldn't I be normal? I should kill myself then I won't be anyone's problem anymore.* These thoughts inside my head kept repeating.

*No one will accept me as I am.* I felt alone. *No one will even care If I'm gone.* I tried to undo what I had done. I asked to stay with the Grahams, but the damage and the hurt was done. There was no way of coming back from that -*I fucked up!* I had often thought about ending my life. What did I really have to live for? I had no friends, my mum and dad didn't want me, I felt pushed aside and rejected by my own family – *so why the fuck was I ever born?*

Everyone was out, I was home alone for the next four hours, so it was now or never. *Just have the guts and do it!* Brian never used to lock his ute when it was parked out the back, on the farm you never had to. I saw the rope bundled up on the seat of the passenger side. I took the rope and walked down to the hay shed. I climbed up to the top of the haystack and tied a knot that I had learnt from going to scouts around a wooden beam that supported the tin roof of the shed. My heart was pounding in my chest and tears streamed down my face as I sobbed. With the dangling rope, I tied it tight around my neck.

I was faced with the final decision. I started an inner dialogue with myself. *'Do I end it all right here?' 'Will it hurt?' 'I'll be ending my miserable existence anyway.'* I took a deep breath in through my nose and slowly exhaled through my mouth, eyes closed, a technique taught in drama class to help calm our nerves before a performance. Then, I suddenly felt calm. I felt numb inside. I stared straight ahead blankly, no expression on my face, no more thoughts racing in my head. Just quiet. As I closed my eyes, I could hear the birds chirping in the background and the trees rustling with the wind. It sounded so peaceful. The sound of my heart pounding in my chest was like a beat to a drum. I stood there for a few minutes. Eyes still closed. Listening to the peaceful sounds around me and the beating of the heart. *This is it! Goodbye.* I bent my knees and lowered myself down, feeling the rope tighten around my neck. *One, two three.* I leant forward and fell off the hay bale. I was hanging. As my body started to fight, my legs were kicking, my body thrashing around. I opened my eyes and started to panic! *Oh, Fuck! Fuck!* I began to regret my decision. I desperately tried to get my feet back on the hay bales, but they kept slipping off. Every time I tried to get my feet back on the hay bales, the rope around my neck tightened. I was choking. I could feel myself become dizzy as the blood was being cut off from my brain.

Hands gripping on the rope around my neck, trying to slip my fingers in between my neck and the rope, but the rope was too tight. *Please, God, I've made a mistake I don't want to die!* I could feel my eyes bulging out of my head. I started to see stars. *I'm so fucked!* I thought to myself. Suddenly, I heard a loud crack! I could feel myself free falling to the ground. Bang! I landed on my arse and back as I hit the ground. I was hit in the head by the wooden beam that had just given way; it had snapped in half as it was rotten inside.

I shit myself! I couldn't believe I tried to hang myself. As I came too, I quickly loosened the rope from around my neck. Gasping for air and coughing trying to suck in air into my lungs. Once I could breathe, I felt relief. I checked my head for blood. There was none. Just a bump. I untied the rope from the broken beam and wound it up the way I found it and put it back in the passenger side of Brian's ute.

There was a storm that night, and everyone thought the damage to the hay shed roof was caused by the wind. I didn't tell anyone that I had tried to kill myself. When Joan questioned the red mark on my neck, I said it was from the horse's lead. Joan seemed to buy my lie. Lying in bed that night, my neck and throat were sore, I felt like I had been punched in the throat and it hurt to swallow. I was angry with myself. *I can't even kill myself, right!* That incident scared me, and I wouldn't be trying that again. I'd have to find another way. The next day I felt remorse. I thought of who would have found me if that beam hadn't of broken. Joan's mum Nanna was always at the farm first thing in the morning, and she would have made the gruesome discovery. Nanna! Poor Nanna!

The weeks after I tried to take my own life, I became withdrawn, kept to myself and decided to stay out of trouble in the hope that things would get back to normal. I felt lost. I had a secret that I couldn't tell anyone. My gay secret was one of the main reasons I thought I had thrown a grenade and blown up the relationship with the family that loved and cared for me for the past five-and-a-half years. I feared their rejection, so it was a self-preservation thing. I hurt them, and I was sorry, but it was too late. My sadness turned to anger. My anger turned to self-loathing and feeling like my life was out of control. I started to become self-destructive, and the only way I knew to release the pain I was feeling, the pain that I was good at hiding in front of others, was to start self-harming.

I was angry. Angry at my social worker. Devastated and fucked off that my own family rejected me. Pissed off with myself for hurting the ones that gave a damn. In denial that I was gay. Disappointed that my previous suicide attempt failed and annoyed that I didn't have the guts to try it again! The intrusive thoughts bombarded my head.

*You're a worthless piece of fucking shit!*

*No one wants you!*

*Your mum and dad don't give a fuck about you!*

*You were a mistake!*

*Everybody hates a faggot!*

*Just have the guts and just die!*

"FUCK OFF!" I would tell my own voice that I heard in my head. The thoughts mainly came at night, and I often had trouble sleeping. There were many nights I would howl myself to sleep into my pillow so no one else could hear. I wanted to suffer in silence. *I deserved it.*

I couldn't regulate my emotions, and I felt a wave of emotions of sadness, guilt, feeling worthless, hatred towards myself and back to anger. I wanted to hurt myself and at the same time, release the pain and gain some control. It started when things weren't going so great at school or at home when I was living with the Graham's. I started making myself throw up after dinner. It wasn't painful, just force a couple of fingers down your throat and make yourself sick. Easy! I had tried cutting my thigh once with a knife, the pain release felt good, but each cut was too noticeable, so I chose the other option. Punishing myself by inducing vomiting released my pain, and I could keep that more secret. I was becoming bulimic.

# CHAPTER 18

# MENTALLY LOSING CONTROL

Joan was in two minds about ending the placement. After the rejection from my family, I had begged her to let me stay. During a visit with Sally, Joan was upset as her heart was telling her to stick with the placement, but her head was telling her it should end. The rest of the family were no help to her in making a decision as they would all go along with what Joan wanted. Having the burden of making this decision must have been a massive burden for her to do alone.

*23/04/1993: Home visit to Joan and Brian Graham*

*Joan very upset during visit-heart telling her to stick with placement but head telling her it should end. Joan not wanting to have placement continue and have it 'blow up', then having no relationship with Shane. The Grahams would like to continue having Shane over for holidays and weekends.* **Sally Conway – Social Worker**

### 27/04/1993: Match for Shane with Gina.

*Gina happy to consider placement with Shane and would like to organise an introduction Friday afternoon.* **Sally Conway – Social Worker**

### 29/04/1993: P/C to DHS worker Liz McDonald

*Informed Liz that placement with the Grahams was ending and that we were about to start an introduction with another foster mother. Liz will arrange for the monthly case planning meeting to be brought forward for early next week.* **Sally Conway – Social Worker**

### 30/04/1993: Intro Shane to Gina Smith

*Shane very sullen and angry – didn't want to meet Gina and refused to make eye contact with either Gina or myself when asked questions. Gina made it clear to Shane that she would be happy for him to give it a go with her.* **Sally Conway – Social Worker**

### 06/05/1993: Home visit to the Grahams and Shane

*Informed the Grahams and Shane that after consultation with the Department of Health and Human Services (DHHS) we had decided to end the placement. Shane furious but did agree to give it a go with Gina and we arranged for Shane to spend Friday night to Saturday with Gina. Grahams are quite angry that the decision had been taken from them. However, the previous fortnight they decided Shane should leave and I feel they were no longer capable of making a decision as Brian and Joan appeared to have different opinions of what should happen.* **Sally Conway – Social Worker**

There was no other choice. I did consider running away, but where would I go? I didn't have any other option, and I didn't want to end up homeless at fourteen. So, I reluctantly went along with the department's decision to rehouse me. I thought to move to a new carer could go in my favour, so I thought I would manipulate the situation and see how lenient she was. Would she let me do what I wanted? I was moving to Cranbourne. Gina only lived 5 minutes from the bus stops. Getting to places on my own would be easier than being on the Graham's farm in which I had to rely on someone to drive me places so I couldn't just do what I wanted. But maybe I could start with this new placement.

### 10/05/1993: Phone call to Gina

*Weekend with Shane went well- Gina stated that he was on his best behaviour. However, Liz (DHS worker) did mention that Shane greeted her with a list of demands (i.e. Wanting to go roller skating every Friday night, not having to ask permission to go somewhere- Shane told Gina, 'I'm old enough to do what I want now'). There will need to be some be negotiating around these issues. Gina is happy for Shane to have dinner with her Wednesday night and that he could take the opportunity to start moving his things.* **Sally Conway – Social Worker**

*11/05/1993: Phone call to Joan and Shane*

*Shane agreed to have dinner with Gina Wednesday night – he wants to change schools. Cranbourne Secondary College may be participating in the Rock Eisteddfod this year. Shane has also auditioned and won a part in a play with the Hampton Park Amateur Theatre Group.* **Sally Conway – Social Worker**

I tried to find a distraction from the mess I had created. I auditioned for a new theatre company, and I won the leading cast role in a romantic comedy, which was written by one of the company's founders. I played a straight football star who was about to get married to his fiancé only to find out he was gay and ended up leaving his fiancé for another guy! Ironic wasn't it since I was struggling with my own sexuality, so I played that role well.

I went and had dinner at Gina's. She lived in a two-bedroom unit in Cranbourne. Gina was a smoker and smoked inside and the place smelt of cigarettes, I was a casual smoker, but I hated the smell, but I soon got used to it. Gina made a roast chicken with roasted potatoes and vegetables. We talked about her house rules and having mutual respect for each other. We also came to the negotiation that I would receive $10 a week for mowing the backyard lawn once a fortnight and putting out the bins once a week. It had been a few weeks since I had the urge to purge my food again, but that night at Gina's I felt that urge. After dinner, I excused myself to go to the toilet and stuck my fingers down my throat and brought up what I had just eaten. On my knees head facing the toilet bowl, I felt a release from the pain I was feeling. The same release you would get from cutting

I would get from purging. I rinsed my mouth out at the basin and walked back out to the table. I don't know if Gina heard me, I tried to be as quiet as I could. Purging was going to be challenging to keep a secret as I was moving into a smaller place.

**13/05/1993: Phone Conversation with Joan**
*Shane had dinner with Gina last night – seemed to go ok. The family are all very upset about the situation of Shane leaving. Joan wondering if Shane will really want to stay in touch as he seems to have plenty of other activities in his life. I think Joan is feeling quite rejected by Shane.* **Sally Conway – Social Worker**

Saturday 16th May 1993 was my last night with the family that I had been with for the past six years. Michelle and her husband Greg, Leanne and her husband Mark, came over to join us all for a family dinner to say goodbye. Paul didn't stay long; he had a girlfriend, and every night after dinner, he would go to her house. I think Paul was affected the most, out of Scott and Paul, and even though Paul would give me a hard time sometimes, I had a stronger bond with him. Paul gave me a quick hug goodbye, wished me luck, and then left. I could feel tears welling up, so I went to the toilet and sobbed. I loved having big brothers and to see that I really hurt Paul made me feel like a worthless piece of shit. The urge to purge came back and I gave into it to punish myself and to release the pain, which that feeling of release started to become addictive. I couldn't stop.

Sunday was the day that it was time to leave the Grahams for good. Joan and I didn't say much to each other during the car ride to my new home in Cranbourne. I felt if I spoke that I would break down and cry, so I pushed my emotions deep down, and that probably made me seem cold-hearted. Thinking back if I could have shown my feelings, maybe that would have shown Joan that I did love them and I was sad to leave, then Joan maybe wouldn't have felt entirely rejected by me. I had my clothes all packed in black garbage bags, and I looked like I had just been released from prison. Joan didn't stay long; we said our goodbyes, and she left. I remember sitting in my new room having this out-of-body experience like this was all a bad dream. But it wasn't. This was my new reality. I did this.

My new foster carer, Gina, was in her fifties and was friendly and tried her best to form a bond with me, but I was too angry to accept her. The loss I felt from leaving home I had known for the past six years was unfathomable, and the rejection I felt from my own family was like a deep wound that would not heal. I was angry at my family, Sally, my social worker, the Grahams, but most of all, I was mad at myself. With so much loss and abandonment, I have felt throughout my life, I was determined to not let Gina in, so I kept her at arm's length.

On my birthday Gina made me a roast dinner with a chocolate mud cake as my birthday cake. I know she was trying to make my birthday special, cheer me up, but I fell deeper into depression as I had only previously spent birthday dinners at the Grahams. I don't even think I thanked her for the effort. After dinner I went to the toilet and threw it all up. I didn't deserve a birthday. I helped Gina do the dishes without saying a word and then went to bed. That weekend I was in my bedroom, and I could overhear Gina talking to her son in the driveway.

"He hates me" Gina said.

I felt terrible; I didn't hate her. I hated myself, and I didn't want to get close to anyone. My mental health was declining.

I became irritable, moody, isolative, I was purging after every meal now, and I started to be verbally aggressive towards Gina. I don't know how I got a job in the middle of the recession, but I ended up getting a casual job at the Cranbourne KFC. I was earning money on my own for the first time.

My shifts were after school and some weekends, which got me out of the house and something to do. I would get into more and more disagreements with Gina, and when I got angry, it was like I disassociated as I had never been verbally aggressive or violent before. I would swear at Gina calling her a fucking cunt and a bitch whenever we would have an argument. I didn't recognise myself, I wasn't well, I couldn't regulate my emotions or anger, I was depressed, and I had an eating disorder.

### 05/07/1993: Phone Call from Gina

*Said that Shane has become verbally aggressive towards her, swearing and yells at her. Gina also a bit concerned that Shane may be bulimic – he threw up after dinner Saturday, and he has taken off to the bathroom straight after eating on more than one occasion. Gina confronted Shane about it, and Shane admitted to doing it (throwing up his food after meals. Shane said to Gina 'I just put my fingers down my throat – it makes me feel better'). Shane said he used to do this at the Grahams too.* **Sally Conway – Social Worker**

### 06/07/1993: Phone Call to Liz –DHHS worker

*Referral has gone into the Adolescent Placement Unit at the Cheltenham office to discuss independent living options for Shane and to address Gina's concerns that Shane may be Bulimic.* **Sally Conway – Social Worker**

I told Sally I wanted to move out and live independently, but I had only turned fifteen. Sally asked me about Gina's concerns about me throwing up my food after meals. I got defensive and angry. "Gina's a nosy bitch who needs to mind her own business!" I yelled. I told Sally that I was just feeling sick at the time, and I hadn't been making myself sick at all. Sally suggested that I go into hospital for a while as I clearly wasn't well. "Get fucked!" I told her, "I'm not mentally ill, I'm just pissed off!" Sally then offerd counselling, and I just scoffed at her, 'I don't need to talk to anyone! I just wanna be left alone!'

### 29/07/1993: Phone Call from Gina

*Gina was upset. Shane told her this morning that he wished he had the guts the kill her weeks ago! This was said after a silent patch since Monday. I told Gina that she didn't have to put up with this and that maybe we should organise another place for Shane to go. Gina agreed. Gina said that this placement was not doing Shane or herself any good. Gina was anxious. Shane may soon resort to physical violence as he seems quite out of control. Gina stated that she has had a lock put on her bedroom door for her own safety.* **Sally Conway – Social Worker**

My empty threats had really frightened Gina. I wouldn't have hurt her. But she was right in the fact I was feeling out of control like I was free falling with no net to catch me. I had thought of killing myself again, but after my last attempt, I was too scared to try again. Sally had me introduced to workers Pat and Fran at Wesley Central Mission in Dandenong. I was assessed to see if I was suitable to move into a new 'Young Men's House' Lead Tenant accommodation they were opening in a month.

A Lead Tenant is a live-in volunteer whose primary role is to mentor, support and help create a positive environment for young tenants living in the home together. Lead Tenants have their rent and utility bills taken care of. As a resident, I would pay rent which also covered utilities, but I would have to buy my own groceries. This arrangement was available for youth that needed support while learning how to live independently and provide youth accommodation who were at risk of homelessness from the ages sixteen to eighteen.

My mental health was deteriorating, I wasn't showering regularly, skipping school, staying in bed all day, purging and still verbally abusing Gina if she confronted me. Sally had to take drastic action. I needed to be moved. I was moved to Yallum House in Dandenong the next day. On the way to Yallum, Sally took me to Hampton Park Secondary College to collect my school report. Besides everything that had been going on this last term, I surprisingly passed the third term of Year Ten!

Yallum was a house for male adolescents aged from twelve to eighteen years who were expressing difficulties in behaviour. I stayed there for four weeks while I waited for the Young Men's House to be set up. At Yallum, a psychologist named Ben would come to the house twice a week, and we had to have sessions with him. The sessions with Ben helped me. I had stopped purging; I began to feel happier and less angry. He gave me worksheets on how to regulate my emotions and gave me strategies that would help when I felt anger, sadness, the urge to purge or was feeling distressed. The plan that he gave me is what I advise my clients now as a mental health nurse to use, called Mindfulness.

Ben explained Mindfulness as something we can practice by maintaining a moment-by-moment awareness of our thoughts, feelings, bodily sensations, and surrounding environment, through a gentle, nurturing lens. I remember him telling me that when we practice mindfulness, our thoughts tune into what we're sensing in the present moment rather than rehashing the past or imagining the future. I would practice this daily, sitting outside under a large tree in the backyard. Using mindfulness helped me calm my thoughts, and I started to think more positively about the future.

I was only a week away before being released from Yallum and moving to my new home. I hadn't seen any of my own family since I moved from the Grahams. When I was struggling at Gina's no one called or visited or invited me over. They were all given my address when I moved, so during that time, I felt I had no one in my life. One of the workers called me into the kitchen, and she handed me an envelope addressed to me. When I opened up the envelope and pulled the folded piece of paper out, I saw it was a letter from my Sally, my foster care worker.

*August 19, 1993*

*Dear Shane,*

*It must feel like you've travelled down a very rocky road over the past 5 months. Let's hope the journey becomes a bit smoother shortly!*

*Shane, it must have taken great courage to decide to leave the Grahams and ask to live with your relatives. It must also have been very disappointing when these plans were not realised. A further source of sadness must have been felt with the decision to end the placement with the Grahams. That decision involved Joan, Brian, the staff at the foster care and me. It was a difficult decision to make for all concerned and one which you probably believed we "got wrong".*

*Shane, I still believe that to have stayed with the Grahams would have been hard for everyone. Perhaps you can understand how hurt they felt when you 'rejected' them – I believe this would have eventually led to an erosion of trust of each other. I also think that your desire for more freedom would have ultimately caused some problems between you and the Grahams.*

*I am sorry that the placement with Gina did not work out for you. I had hoped that this placement would allow you to develop your skills before independent living. However, I respect the fact that you felt this placement was just not right for you.*

*So now it's time to look to the future. This must be both an exciting and scary time. Shane, I hope your plans to live semi-independently work out and remember, you don't have to do it all on your own. Some people can provide help and support, including the Grahams.*

*The skills I believe you already have which will help you include: determination (after all, you got a job in the midst of a recession and high unemployment!), excellent school achievement, ability to seek out necessary information and work towards your goals, lots of interests, friendliness and a positive attitude about the future.*

*As you are aware, I am no longer going to be involved as your 'case worker'. However, I would be pleased if you gave me a call sometime and let me know how you are going. Also, if there is any information that you need and think I might have on file, please call me.*

*Best wishes,*

**Sally Conway, Social Worker**


Eighteen is the current age when you 'age out of the foster care system' and eighteen is still seen as too young. I aged out at sixteen and my wardship lapsed and was not renewed by the courts. I was on my own now. When I look back, I see how lucky I was. Not many other teenagers are that lucky. I don't know how but I managed to have ongoing support from Sally Conway, Oz Child and the caseworkers at Wesley Mission.

I was spiralling out of control feeling lost, confused, scared, angry and alone. I don't know how I managed to find the strength to jump out of this circle of self-harm and self-destruction. Rereading the letter from Sally still brings me to tears today. Maybe I still have some remorse for how I acted like a teenager, how no one gave up on me even when I hurt them with my vile words, I spReyed at them when I couldn't control my anger.

This was it, I got what I wished for. I started to receive a student study allowance - 'Austudy' which was $485 a fortnight from the Government agency Centrelink to live on. With a new caseworker named Ben, I was lucky to have the support and the new 'Men's House' to move into. A lot of teenagers that age out of the foster care system aren't so lucky. Many that must leave care once they turn eighteen become homeless, unemployed, addicted to drugs and alcohol, involved in the criminal justice system or become parents within the first year of being exited from care. Most of us lacked the skills to take care of ourselves, and at sixteen, for me, this was going to be sink or swim.

# CHAPTER 19

# BECOMING INDEPENDENT

My stay at Yallum House ended, and the Young Men's House in North Dandenong was up and running, and I was its first tenant. Fran, one of the Wesley Mission social workers, drove me to K-Mart where we stocked the house with a new toaster, kettle, plates, glasses, utensils etc. I was excited to be finally living semi-independently. I was sixteen, and I had gotten what I wanted. My wardship had lapsed and was not renewed, I had no adults to tell me what to do or make decisions for me, I was on my own. But what's that saying Joan used to say? *The grass isn't always greener on the other side of the fence...* I'll talk about that later.

Matt, a social worker student, aged twenty-three, moved in as our Lead Tenant and was chosen as a volunteer by Wesley Mission, to provide mentorship and support. Matt was tall, thin with spiky dark brown hair that he dyed red in parts. Matt was a good-looking guy who was very kind to me, and of course, I developed a crush on him. But Matt was straight and way too old for me! Matt was a member of the Salvation Army Church, and he went to Church every Sunday morning. Matt once asked if I wanted to go, but I politely declined, telling him I wasn't a church kind of person. He didn't judge, and with his kind, the warm smile said, "That's cool maybe one day".

At the beginning of term four of year ten, I changed schools from Hampton Park Secondary College to Doveton Secondary College, where my cousins Tania and Leonie went. Tania and I were in the same year level, and Leonie was in Year Eight. I was so excited to be able to see my cousins every day. And, I settled into independent living too comfortably.

I had to quickly learn how to manage my money, buy groceries and cook from myself. Lucky for me that Joan had taught me how to cook, so I had no trouble in that department. The money management I wasn't so good at and would always be broke two days before my next pay. Rent money was automatically deducted from my Austudy payments, and the rest I could use at my leisure.

I decided that I wanted to pursue my singing, dancing and acting career, so I auditioned and was accepted into the Johnny Young Talent School (JYTS) in Richmond. Every Thursday night I caught the train from Dandenong to Richmond station after school to make my singing and dancing classes. The teens in my classes and their parents to pay for their lessons, where I had to pay for them on my own. I was living the life I wanted with no rules and not having to live up to anyone else's expectations, I could be who I wanted to be.

Tania and I had the same group of friends. I was the new kid but made friends quickly at Doveton Secondary College. I had no troubles with bullies and Tania was like my best friend at school. Unlike when I was at Hampton Park, I had guy friends. I became close mates with a guy called Dean. He was tall, played basketball and a fit body. And yes, I developed a crush on him but never told anyone. I had never experienced having a lot of guy friends, so it was a little weird, to begin with, but it didn't take long to get used to having friends. Starting a new school, you could start a clean slate as no one knew who you were before.

I had joined the JYTS agency and auditioned and won a lead role in an educational video. When I got the call from the agency, I was so excited. I took a day off school to do the shoot. I was playing a troubled teen that had self-doubt and a bad attitude. We filmed in a pool hall in Richmond, and I worked for 8 hours, my first professional acting gig. *I have reached my dreams,* I thought to myself. I had quit my casual job at KFC, so I had more time to pursue acting roles. In December, we had the Young Talent Time Christmas Concert in a theatre in Camberwell. I had invited my old Social Worker Sally, Joan and Brian and Ben, my new caseworker at Wesley Mission. Again, Joan and Brian made an effort to support me, but my own family couldn't make it.

After Christmas, we got a new housemate. His name was Zac; he was 17 years old and had been sleeping rough in the streets for the past year. One Sunday night I was trying to get to sleep for my new year of school, I was starting Year Eleven, and he had around 15 of his mates around hanging in the lounge room playing loud music and smoking in the house. Matt was trying to get them to stop smoking and turn down the music.

Zac and his friends weren't being very co-operative, and by this stage, I'd had enough- I was raging! I came flying out of my room and screamed at them all, "Get the fuck out of this house!" They all just looked at me in shock, and then they got up and left once they saw I wasn't joking. The next day I wanted to play my favourite girl, band SWV's CD, and I couldn't find it. It had been there last night. Then I realised that one of Zac's friends must have taken it. Matt must have told the staff at Wesley Mission what when on, and the next day Zac was gone.

I had passed Year Eleven, and now I was in my final year of high school. Everyone was turning eighteen, and there were a lot of parties that year. It was something about bonding over drunken party weekends that made the entire Year Twelve level really close. I had only turned seventeen in June and had to use a fake ID to go to the nightclubs in Dandenong. On Saturday nights I would go out with my two girl pals, Lisa and Rebecca to the Nu Hotel and The Storm night clubs. My fake ID was some random eighteen-year-old Asian dude's learners permit, and I used to get in with that all the time. We would crash at Lisa's house in Endeavour Hills and on Sunday morning, eat ice cream and watch Video Hits as we rested our hungover heads. I felt brave, and I came out to the girls.

"I'm gay" I said. They both looked at each other and laughed.

"We know Shane, just waiting for you to realise it".

It was such a relief not to have this secret hanging over my shoulders and liberating that my friends didn't care.

Now our final year at school was ending, it was time to decide what we were going to do with our lives. I wanted to go to Deakin University to major in Drama and Contemporary Dance. Upon registration, we were given numbers to stick on the front of our tops. My number was 19. I was wearing black dance pants and a black singlet top. After learning the choreography, we were split into two groups to perform in front of the panel of interviewers. I tried not to let the nerves consume me, but I was in the 2nd group and watching the first group dance made me feel more nervous.

One guy caught my eye- number 78. He looked like he had done ballet all his life. He was mesmerising to watch. Number 78 was tall and masculine with messy black hair, and when he lifted up his arms the bottom of his stomach was revealed, and I could see his pelvic lines, what I call 'man lines' and are a real turn on. He moved so strong, with purpose and precision that he made the choreography seem so effortless. I was in awe. When the time came for the groups to swap number 78 walked past me, "Nice job" I said. Number 78 not saying anything smiled at me shyly as we walked past each other.

I made the final cut of the audition process, now it was up to what score I got for my VCE exams. The time had come for our 'muck up' day, our last day of high school ever! The jock boys planned the night. We met at the school at 3am wearing cartoon masks in case we got caught. The jock boys dug out of the football oval 'VCE 1995' while the rest of us threw toilet paper over the trees and in front of the main office. With the excitement and adrenaline pumping through our veins, we were all like wild animals let loose in a zoo. When the teachers arrived in the morning, the Jock boys water bombed them, and the rest of us threw flour at them.

The teachers were expecting that we would do something crazy, as most of them brought a spare change of clothes. It was all a lot of fun until two of the guys went too far. They targeted one of the older female teachers that nobody really liked, and they carried over a bin full of water and tipped it over her head. She was gasping for air, and in shock from the cold water, I thought she was going to have a heart attack! Once she was drenched with water, they tipped a whole bag of flour over her head. She wasn't impressed, furious that she was wet and covered in flour, she got into her car and sped off to go home. The principal came out and told the guys off for going too far. That kind of dampened the mood.

It seemed like forever to wait for the results of our exams and the university 'enter' scores. I thought I had done OK in the exams and I was off to Deakin University to study drama and contemporary dance. When they arrived, I was shocked to see that I didn't get the score I needed. I was devastated. I called the coordinator of the drama and dance department to see if I could still have a place in the program because I had made the final cut of the auditions. But without the right entrance score, I couldn't be considered. 'Try again next year, she said.

The following year I was about to turn eighteen, and my time of supportive living was coming to an end, and I would have to move out. My relationship with Joan and Brian had significantly improved, and I asked if I could go back home. Joan was reluctant at first, but then after discussing it with Brian and Sally, my past social worker, they agreed to have me back as a private boarder.

The following year was 1996, and I attempted my VCE, year 12 again to try and better my score to get into university. I was glad that Rebecca was going to repeat her VCE as well to get into a course she had missed out on the previous year. So at least I had a friend.

When you turn eighteen, your time at Johnny Young Talent School came to an end. I joined an adult acting agency called 'Linda's Rising Stars' in Richmond. I started working as an extra for Neighbours, a student in the background, before getting featured in extra and speaking, bit part roles.

I started getting type-cast as a bad boy or in gangs. One role I got was for Channel 9's Good Guys Bad Guys starring Marcus Graham where I played a private schoolboy in a gang lead by a rich kid drug dealer. I auditioned for more substantial roles, but it's a hard gig with a lot of competition out there.

In December 1996, I won a small role as a wannabe DJ volunteer for the ABC's TV series 'Raw FM'. The plot of the show was about the lead character, Granger (Dominic Purcell), a DJ at commercial radio station Rock FM, who is fired from his job, so he and his long-time friends Robert and the blind Zelda (Nadine Garner) decide to start their own independent radio station. However, they are completely unprepared for the number of kids who show up wanting to be DJs — many of whom are quite lazy. They hire staff from a group of volunteers and have a launch party. In subsequent episodes, we find out more about each of the staff as different episodes focus on different characters.

The year went quickly, I was back in a home environment, and I didn't have to fend for myself, and I could concentrate more on my studies. On my eighteenth birthday, Joan took me into the city to see Beauty and the Beast the Musical playing at the regent theatre. This was a real bonding moment, and I was touched by her acknowledgement of my interest in musical theatre and a special memory that we both shared.

The time came around again to see what enter score I achieved from repeating Year Twelve and which university I had gotten into if any. I think I paced up and down the driveway waiting for the postman to arrive with our mail. When I finally got the letters, I quickly opened it up. I was too nervous to look, but I didn't go through another year of high school not to know. I opened the letter, my hands were shaking, I looked down, and the letter started off with 'Congratulations! You have been accepted into the Bachelor of Arts at Deakin University – Warrnambool.'

*Where the fuck is Warrnambool?*

# CHAPTER 20

# WARRNAMBOOL

Summer break 1997, I worked for Brian. When Brian retired from the police force, he and Paul started a fencing business. I would work on weekends and school holidays for extra cash. Even when I left home, they never turned their backs on me. I was the only one in the immediate family to be going to university.

The others had gone straight into the workforce and brought their houses and cars. Having assets and financial stability was their dream, but I was more of a free spirit. My biological parents didn't have much education, and I didn't want to end up like them, I wanted something better for my life. I loved the arts, and I wanted to experience University life before settling down in a career. Plus, Joan suggested that it would be good to have something to fall back on if acting and dancing didn't work out.

A month before the uni semester was about to start, it was time to enrol and choose your major. Now, in the '90s there was no such thing as enrolling online, you had to physically go to the university and enrol in person with the guidance of an enrolment officer. So, Joan, Brian and Grandpa (Brian's Dad) decided to drive me up to Warrnambool for a road trip. We drove along the Great Ocean Road, and the scenic beach views of the cliffs were breathtaking. I had never seen the Great Ocean Road, and I will forever hold this trip close to my heart.

When we arrived at Deakin University, I thought it was a country town because surrounding the university was just paddocks with cows and I didn't realise the main town was only 10 mins down the road. The campus grounds were huge with a golf course and uni bar that overlooked the Hopkins River.

Building A was where I had to enrol and at the entrance was a line of freshly graduated high school students, and you could feel the buzz of excitement in the air. I enrolled in a double major of Graphic Design, Photography & Fine Arts and Public Relations. I intended to complete the first year at Deakin then if my grades were good enough, I could transfer back to Melbourne and enrol in the Contemporary Dance and Drama majors the following year.

The last week of February 1997 was the day I left the comforts of the family home in Devon Meadows to embark on the adventures of my next three years as a University student. This wasn't so daunting as I had already experienced a couple of years living out of home if anything, I was excited to begin a new chapter in my life. I felt proud of myself that I finally had my dreams realised, and I was the only one in my family to be going to university. Joan and Brian drove me into the city to

Southern Cross station, where I was to catch the V-Line train to Warrnambool. As I hugged them both goodbye, Joan handed me an envelope. Inside was a card saying congratulations and a handwritten note telling me how proud they were of me and how far I had come. Also, in the envelope were twenty green $100 bills, a total of $2000!

"This is to help you buy books, art supplies for uni and to help you set yourself up" Joan said.

I teared up and thanked them both, hugged them both again and boarded my train. I made sure I got the window seat so I could wave to them as the train took off. The train started to move, and we waved at each other until I couldn't see them anymore. I was overcome with emotion and started to cry. I felt so lucky and loved.

Joan and Brian had done for me more than my father, or my extended family ever did. They didn't have to, as soon as I moved out and my wardship ended at sixteen they could have just turned their backs on me, but they didn't. I was so grateful for them to me; they were my parents.

The trip to Warrnambool was just a little over three hours. I had fallen asleep and was woken up by the conductor. I had arrived. I had two large suitcases that I wheeled onto the platform. Everyone had left the station, and I thought I was the last one to leave. When I looked up, I saw a tall skinny white dude with light brown hair wearing big round glasses.

We laughed at each other as we said hi, realising how ridiculous we must have looked being the only ones left on the platform struggling with our bags. He got into a taxi, and I walked to my accommodation I had gotten in a panic two weeks ago.

I had planned to live on campus, but I left it too late to apply, and there was no availability, so I caught the train up to Warrnambool for the day two weeks ago to find somewhere to live. I had found a boarding house with a red door, which was the front entrance.

The boarding house wasn't far from the train station and at the end of the main street of Warrnambool's city's centre. As I entered a lady in her fifties greeted me with that warm country smile.

"Welcome, I'm Janet" she smiled as she shook my hand. Janet showed me to my room, which was located towards the back of the house. My room had two single beds and a bunk bed with a desk, chair and lamp. I wheeled my suitcases next to one of the single beds, and she then proceeded to show me the bathrooms, dining area and lounge room. The house was empty.

"Everyone is either at work or at school", Janet said. As she walked me back to my room, Janet said, "Dinner is at 6pm darl, I'll leave you to settle in" and she left. I already felt homesick, but self-soothed reminding myself that uni would start tomorrow and how exciting that would be.

After unpacking, I was feeling extremely hot, the weather was 30 degrees with not a cloud in the bright blue sky. I changed into my shorts and walked down to the surf beach and went for a dip. The water was refreshingly cool as the waves crashed onto my back, I felt rejuvenated. I couldn't believe this coastal town was going to be my home for the next three years.

I had a restless sleep, in a new bed and hot weather with just the fan blowing on me throughout the night, plus with the excitement of starting uni, I only got about 5 hours sleep. I stood under the shower for about half an hour to wake up and then headed to the dining room for breakfast.

I had met a blonde girl named Ella, who was in her twenties and a schoolteacher from Melbourne, completing a teaching contract in Warrnambool. Ella was engaged and would go back to Melbourne every weekend. Ella became my friend in the boarding house, and we would spend nights chatting about our days, life and her fiancé. Ella was near the end of her twelve-month contract and when she left, and I was sad to see her go as she was my only friend in the house.

The first day of uni gave me feelings of anxiety and excitement about what was to come. I caught the uni bus, which only cost 50 cents one way to the campus. When the bus stopped at one of the stops on the main highway, I saw the tall dude that greeted me at the train station yesterday.

"Hi, you were at the station yesterday?" he said.

"Yeah, I was. I'm Shane" I replied.

"Tom" he said as he sat next to me.

After telling each other where we were from and what we were studying, it ended up that we were going to be in the same public relations classes. Tom was studying a triple major in Public Relations, Politics and Philosophy. I was going to be the arty farty student, and he was the real academic.

Tom ended up becoming my best friend and over the years like my brother, a relationship that has lasted over 21 years, where his family became like my second family. Tom was living in a block of flats on Raglan Parade/Princess Highway, sharing with a guy named Heffa, a mechanic that frequented the Bachelor and Spinsters Balls (BNS balls) that are held in rural areas of Australia, and was never home. When Tom saw where

I lived, he thought the boarding house was like an asylum. Tom remembers it as the 'red door' house. Admittedly, when he did come over, he only saw an old man rocking in a chair watching the TV.

A couple of flats up from Tom's was another uni student named Amy, and it just happened she was looking for a flatmate. Tom introduced us, and we hit it off straight away, and the next day I had moved into her front room. Amy was in the second year at uni and was from the country town of Colac about 2 hours from Warrnambool.

Amy was a largish beautiful girl with a bubbly personality, and the three of us became great friends. I hit the jackpot with housemates because Amy loved to cook and would make me dinner every night. My favourite dish of Amy's was her meatballs and gravy with mashed potatoes and veggies.

We would make sure there was enough for Tom as the poor guy was in the first apartment eating weetbix, muffins and sausage rolls as he didn't know how to cook. An example of this was when Tom had borrowed one of Amy's plastic Tupperware bowls to heat up fried rice he had brought from Coles.

Instead of putting the bowl in the microwave, he put the plastic bowl in the oven. Amy and I could smell burning plastic from our unit, which was 2 doors up from Tom's. We both raced down to Tom's, and there he was trying to save his rice and couldn't understand why the bowl had melted in the oven. We still laugh about it to this day; Tom has never lived this down, and now I've told the world.

Every Sunday, Tom would walk past in a suit to go to Church. Tom was brought up in the Christian faith and in an evangelist church back in Melbourne. Every time he would pass our unit

Amy, and I would yell out "Churchin!" and Tom would reply with "Sexin!" and this was our running joke. The first semester went by quick and Tom, and I had gone back to our family homes for a few weeks.

While I was home, I worked with Brian, Paul and Scott building fences. During this time, something hit me, like a calling or yearning to check out Tom's church. I had slept on that thought, and the next day at work it came back, "Try Tom's Church" my voice said to me. When I returned to Warrnambool, I told Tom about my yearning and the voice in my head telling I need to check out his church. The following Sunday, I went with Tom to his Church, and I was pleasantly surprised.

During the first service, I felt closer to God. It's hard to explain, but I just felt at ease, like everything was going to be OK. The church youth were from uni, and we were all around the same age, some a year or so older than me. Our pastor Wayne, and his wife Hanna were both in their 30's with a two-year-old son Peter and another one on the way. It wasn't long before I joined the music team lead by Hanna, and I felt like I belonged. The youth of the church was Wayne's work-force, or walking group when he wanted to get fit, he had a group of young men, and he knew how to keep us occupied so we didn't get into drinking and having casual sex like all the other uni students.

The day I gave my heart to Jesus, a group of us went surfing at a beach that really wasn't meant for novice swimmers like myself. That day I tested God and said that if he were authentic, then he would have to show me for me to really believe. I knew I'd felt him before, but I just wanted to be sure. Well, big mistake. I came off my board, and then as I came up for air, another wave smashed on top of me pushing me under the water as the force tumbled me around like a washing machine. When I finally found my way back to the top and gasped for air, another wave came, then another and another, I thought I was going to drown that day. I came close.

Then I felt someone drag me up out of the water fling me up onto a surfboard. It was Ro. Ro was from the Dandenong area and was a couple years older than me, studying nursing at the uni with Al, another guy at the church. Ro was born in Cape Town South Africa, and his family had migrated to Australia when he was young. Ro was a good-looking black guy with a charismatic charm that instantly made you like him. That day he saved my life, and I think that's when I developed a crush on him. I struggled with this because I would pRey for God to heal me and make me like all the other guys – straight. I didn't want to be gay! I didn't want to be different! For once I just wanted to fit in!


Christmas 1997 My foster parents were away for the holiday's so Tom invited me back to his families for Christmas. Toms family consisted of his mother Milly, his older sister Lilly and the oldest sister Kate. Kate lived in Canberra at the time working in Public Relations, and Lilly was at Tafe studying fine art. Toms family are unique, and I love them! When there is a problem, they all hash it out there and then. Nothing is held back. When it's all over, it's back to normal again. A Christian family that took me in and made me apart of their family for the last 20 years. They have all been there for me through my good and bad times in my life, with no judgement, just love and understanding.

Milly is an Aboriginal woman, a victim of the stolen generation. Milly was born up in the Northern Territory in the Aboriginal country called Kalkaringi, which is located west of Katherine. Milly and I had similar upbringings in state care, which forged a special bond between us. I consider her my second Mum.

# CHAPTER 21

# PREY THE GAY AWAY

I thought that the day you give your heart to Jesus that your life would become easier. But for me, it just brought all the shit to the surface. Like God was trying to force me to deal with my pain, my demons, my self-hatred, my depression, my lust for boys so I could be cleansed once and for all, a pure image free of sin. I mean that's why Jesus shed his blood on the cross right? To cleanse us of our sins.

At times I felt more disconnected than ever before. I would prey every day for the same thing. *God please, please make me normal.* I felt like he wasn't hearing me, and I didn't under-stand why. Back then didn't understand me, my mental illness or sexuality. I would latch onto the guys at church like Ro, Al and Rich and because of my past, I didn't know how to be friends with guys without falling for them because they showed me kindness and were my type.

I was lonely and mistook friendship for wishing a romantic relationship with straight guys. I never understood this, but I do now. When I was sexually abused by the two teenagers when I was six years old, this skewed my perception of how to have healthy male relationships. I was clearly gay, but I could never accept it. I thought God could heal me, but I was wrong.

I was in my final year of uni, and I had auditioned for Jesus Christ Superstar, produced by the Warrnambool Theatre Production. I won the role of Jesus! Tom and the boys thought it was funny having a Filipino Jesus. This time of my life was so significant. Jesus accepted people from all walks of life, his disciples were the misfits of society, but he accepted and loved them anyway. My walk with God was anthemic as both my spiritual and sexual orientation awakening collided with such a force like dross being drained from the gold.

Trisha, a fellow cast member who played Mary Magdalene, had a gay friend named Toby. Toby was twenty-seven years old, and I was twenty-one at the time. Toby was tall, blond with blue eyes with an athletic figure. He was gorgeous! I felt an instant attraction to him, and I could feel he felt the same way. *God, why are you doing this to me? Eyes on Jesus! Eyes on Jesus!* I would say to myself.

I tried so hard to keep our friendship strictly platonic, but he was sweet and persistent. On the opening night, Toby brought me a bunch of red roses to my dressing room. It was so thoughtful and kind and romantic, but I couldn't give into my desires, I didn't want to sin and have my friends find out I was gay and lose them. I was so gutless. One night, Trish and I went over to his apartment to eat take out and watch a movie. When the movie finished, Trish announced that she was going home as she had to get up early for work the next day. Toby worked in the local bottle shop, so his hours were mainly in the afternoon and evenings.

"Come up here" Toby said lying on the couch.

I lay in front of him while he held me in his arms. His warm body radiated next to mine, and I felt so comfortable there like I should always have been in his arms. My heart was racing a million miles an hour, I could feel it pumping out of my chest. Toby put his hand up my T-shirt and felt my body. I felt anxious at first. Was this wrong? Will I go to hell for this? I struggled with this inner dialogue. Toby's touch felt so good and I could feel my self-getting hard. All I wanted to do was to roll over and kiss him. I turned over to face him, our nose touching while we explored each other's bodies. *Fuck it,* I thought, and I kissed him. Electricity pulsed through my body as this was the first time I had kissed a guy.

"You're full of surprises" Toby said.

I couldn't stop kissing him, his lips were soft, and he was a great kisser. I rolled on top of him, and we undid each other's jeans just enough to see our erect cocks through our jocks. I didn't know what I was really doing. I started rubbing my cock on his as we kissed passionately and then, *oh shit!* I had come in my jocks in less than a few minutes. I felt so embarrassed. Toby laughed. He thought it was cute. He knew he was my first gay experience, and he seemed proud of that. I excused myself and went to the bathroom. I grabbed a handful of toilet paper and wiped the sticky mess from my jocks and washed my cock in the sink.

I stayed over that night. Toby and I fooled around some more, and I experienced my first blow job. He was amazing. I slept peacefully in his arms the entire night. When I awoke, I was riddled with guilt. I had classes in the afternoon, so Toby drove me home.

"I'm sorry, Toby. What we did last night that could never happen again. Can we just be mates?"

"Sure" Toby replied, but I could see he was disappointed.

But every time we hung out, it kept happening because I couldn't control myself. I was hot and cold with Toby, giving him mixed messages.

"Shane I can't keep doing this! I'm falling in love with you. What do you want? There's nothing wrong for being who you are!"

"I'm sorry Toby. I really like you I do. I'm just confused right now."

"I'm not going to be your plaything while you figure things out. Maybe it's best if we cool it while you figure out if you want me or not" Toby said.

I was such a coward! Toby could have been the one, my first love. He was the one that I let get away because I was too afraid to admit to myself who I really was. My church family were too important to me, and I was afraid of losing that. So, I gave up the one person that could have made me happy and loved me. Instead, I told Wayne and agreed to have gay conversion therapy with Hanna's father, Larry. One thing about the therapy that makes me laugh to this day is when Larry got me to close my eyes and imagine the goal posts on a footy field.

"These goal posts are bent, and they resemble you and your sexual feelings towards men. Now, imagine that with God's power, you straighten the poles one by one until they are straight, standing tall again. This is how we can help fix you."

*Um, what the fuck! This is batshit crazy!* I thought, but I went along with it anyway. I stayed in the church for the rest of the year until I moved back to Melbourne to finish my last six months at Deakin to complete the contemporary dance component of my degree. Tom and Marie had gotten engaged, Ro was dating a girl, and I had no one.

I could have had someone great, but I allowed myself to be brainwashed into thinking God could make me straight again. I denied myself who I really was, and I didn't dare to accept that I was gay. I tried to contact Toby, but he had moved, I didn't know where, but if you would ask me what my regret was during that time it would have been denying myself a chance of true love and happiness. I'm gay, and God loves me for who I am.

# CHAPTER 22

# TRAGIC LOSS

Friday the 18th of January 2002, Tim had organised a boys catch up at a restaurant in Box Hill, the suburb Tom and Marie were living now. I met the boys at the restaurant we were going to have dinner at. My mobile phone started ringing. I pulled it out of my pants pocket and saw that it was Joan's brother Uncle John calling. He told me that I needed to come home straight away, but he didn't want to tell me over the phone. I insisted. Reluctantly, he told me that Brian had died this afternoon of a heart attack. My heart sank as it didn't seem real.

I had to tell the boys I had to go and told them all that my foster dad had just died. I drove as fast as I could to get back home, conscious not to get a speeding fine or have a car accident. Tears were flowing down my face, in shock as if I hadn't heard uncle John properly. *No, Brian can't be dead!* When I arrived at the house, the entire family were there, and my heart sank as I realised, I did hear Uncle John properly.

As I entered through the front door, I was greeted and hugged by the extended family, cousins, aunties and uncles. I saw Joan and hugged her as she sobbed on my shoulder. When I was a teenager, Brian had a few strokes and was told to take it easy, but dad wasn't the type of person to sit around all day and do nothing. Leanne came up to me and hugged me "I tried to save him Shane" she said through her tears.

"What happened?" I asked

"I was helping dad do a small fencing job today, and he collapsed. I called the ambulance and then did CPR until the ambulance arrived. But by the time they arrived, Dad was gone."

"Don't blame yourself. You did all you could," I reassured her.

That Friday was a 30-degree day, and the heat must have taken a toll on him. Brian was my Dad in my eyes. I felt more of the loss now losing my foster dad than I did when my biological father 'Rey' died. When Rey died, I didn't feel much at all. But now I have lost two of my fathers, Brian was more influential in my life.

A man that never said the words "I love you" but showed that he loved you in other ways, like never turning his back on me when I moved out of home, or when I came out gay, spending time with me by taking me on drives to Rosebud to get the rejected carrots from the market gardens to feed the cows; and his funny nickname for me 'Frog' (chocolate frog). Never again will I hear dad say, "Hey frog make us a coffee" or hanging out at McDonald's after a hard morning's work when I helped him build the fences on the weekends. It used to annoy the shit out of me when we would watch TV and Brian would channel surf, but I would give anything to see him sitting in his chair watching TV again.

Paul was working that weekend a few hours out of Melbourne, and we didn't want to tell him over the phone. Scott asked me and a couple of the cousins to drive with him to where Paul was working. When we got there, Paul was surprised to see us all. Scott got out of the car and broke the news to him. Paul yelled, cupping his head in disbelief, and Scott comforted him by putting his hand on Paul's shoulder.

The rest of us got out of the car and walked up to where the boys were standing, and when Paul saw me, he pulled me in close and hugged me tightly. Paul and I always had a strong bond. When I was little, I worshipped the ground he walked on, my big brother, my hero. Being only five years apart when we were younger, Scott, and I used to fight. I guess I was like an annoying little brother to him. But as we grew into adulthood, we became closer.

The Sunday afternoon I went to see Tom and Marie to fill them in on what had happened. They were devastated for me. I wanted to honour Dad at his funeral by writing a tribute to him. The words just flowed as I frantically wrote them down on paper, trying to keep up with my mind. Tom put chords to the song so easily, like it was meant to be or something. I titled my tribute song 'Always call you Dad'. That night I found a producer that would record it that night, so we went to his studio and it only took 2 hours to lay it down. A quick edit and mastering and I had my tribute song. I showed Mum and Leanne and they thought it was a perfect song for the funeral.

# Always Call You Dad

V1:      You turned my life around
           When you came into my life
           A gift that I've been given
           To have grown up with you as my Dad
           And I know that you'll always be here with
           And I'll always remember
           Remember, the man you were to me

Ch:     And I thank you for loving me
           And I thank you for giving me
           The best years of my life
           When all is said and done
           It's been an honour to be your son
           And I'll always call you dad

V2:     So many things to say
           That I never got to say
           How much you meant to me
           And I hope that one day
           I'll grow to be the man
           That you wanted me to be

Ch:     And I thank you for loving me
           And I thank you for giving me
           The best years of my life
           When all is said and done
           It's been an honour to be your son
           And I'll always call you dad

*Bridge:* You were my world
And I'm glad to have had you in it
You were my world
And I would change anything for a minute
And I know that you'll always be here with
And I always remember
Remember the man you were to me

Ch:     And I thank you for loving me
And I thank you for giving me
The best years of my life
When all is said and done
It's been an honour to be your son
And I'll always call you dad
Dad.

It has been seventeen years since we lost Brian, my father figure, the one I called Dad. Brian was there for me when Rey wasn't. Brian was the father that never let me down, never turned his back on me when I screwed up, taught me about work ethic, how to trust people again and to never stop trying to better yourself. Joan and Brian (Mum and Dad) gave me a family life that I couldn't get from my biological family.

Everyone else put me in the too hard basket, but not my foster parents, they took me back even when I hurt them by rejecting them, they never rejected me, even after I came out as gay. During my twenties, I started to lose control again. But I believe I survived myself with my special people watching over me from heaven. Nan, Pop and Brian.

# CHAPTER 23

# FIRST TIME ON THE SCENE

It was Christmas night year 2002, and I was twenty-three years old, and I was ready to fully dive into the gay pool. I was nervous and excited at the same time. I had to talk myself into it, '*What do you have to lose?*' I was house sitting an apartment in the Melbourne CBD on Flinders lane at the time, alone, with just the cats to talk to.

After I finally got the courage, I picked up my car keys and drove to Commercial Road in Prahran, which was known for the gay strip in Melbourne. It was still early in the night, about 10pm and I had been reading up on a Gay bar called the X-change Hotel. I didn't think it would be as busy as it was.

There were boys and men everywhere. I guess some gay guys that have been estranged from their disapproving families formed their own family with their friends. So, a night out to celebrate Christmas with mates was the thing to do, and the X-Change Hotel was the place to be. The front bar had guys playing pool, sitting on the leather lounges chatting. I went up to the bar to buy a drink, and the topless muscled barmen served me. He was beautiful! He look about 25 years old, blond wavy hair, blue eyes and flawless tanned skin.

"What will ya have?"

"Ah, a Gin and Tonic Please."

He winked at me and went to make my drink. I couldn't stop staring at his chiselled six-pack. '*He's so sexy.*'

"That's six dollars mate. Are you new here? I haven't seen you around before?" the sexy barman asked.

"Yeah, first time here" I said shyly as I handed him the money.

"Well, I'm Beau. Have a great night" he said with his perfect smile.

"Thanks."

I stood there drinking my drink and felt a bit out of place, and it was probably obvious how awkward I felt. I walked around to the back bar where the dance floor was. Everyone was crowded in front of the stage, waiting for something. I manoeuvred through the crowd up near the front of the stage and leant against the bar. Then suddenly the music changed and out comes a group of men dressed up as women doing an act on stage. They were wonderful and funny, and I just loved watching them. I later learned this was called a drag show. Gay men who loved to dress up as girls, create characters and perform on stage. They were funny and sassy and an important part of gay culture.

Watching the show, I notice a guy standing next to me from the corner of my eye. His back is leaning on the bar. I look over to him, and I catch his eye, and he gives me a smile. I shyly smile back not knowing what to say.

"How's your night?" I felt the warm breath of the guy moving closer to my ear, attempting to initiate conversation.

"Good. I just got here. First time here" I replied, talking into his ear.

"I'm Tyler" he smiled. I noticed his cute little dimples. My eyes examined him. His head was shaved, and he was wearing a black singlet top. He wasn't muscly. He was average in build, taller than me, and I found him cute as hell.

"Shane" I said, smiling back at him. I felt a rush of butterflies hit my stomach. I was nervous and excited at the same time. Some cute guy is talking to me. I didn't know what else to say.

"Who you here with?" Tyler asked.

*No one. On my own. I better explain, or he'll think I'm a loser.* 'I've just started to explore the gay scene. Not out long' I said.

"That's cute" he said.

I awkwardly smiled at him. *I'm such a newbie. I want to kiss him, but I was too scared to make the first move.* I turned away to watch the rest of the drag show. I kept taking sneaky glances at him watching the show. Tyler must have been doing the same. Just like in the movies, we both turned to look at each other and then it happened. Tyler moved closer and kissed me. I was timid at first. My heart beating fast. Tyler pulled me in closer to him, his arms wrapped around my waist. I placed my arms around his back as he massaged my tongue with his.

*He is such a great kisser...*

When we finally came up for air Tyler looked into my eyes, placing his arms over my shoulders and said, "If I didn't have a boyfriend, I'd take you home right now."

"Wait, what?" I said in shock.

"It's OK. I am in an open relationship. My boyfriend and I have an understanding" Tyler said.

I was new to this, so I guess there was a lot to learn about the gay culture. I didn't quite understand why you would have an open relationship if you were in a loving relationship? Not my thing, I'd get too jealous. Tyler gave me his number before he left, but I just didn't feel right calling him so, I didn't.

I had gotten the courage to come out to my foster family, and to my surprise, it was no big deal.

'We already knew, we were just waiting for you to realise it,' Mum, Michelle and Leanne said.

'It's about time!' Scott said.

'I don't care! But why do you wanna play with other guys doodles when you have your own? Paul joked.

'I'm just disappointed that you didn't feel you could come to me earlier, Leanne said.

Are you serious? I thought. All that angst I felt when I was fifteen, trying to kill myself, leaving home and all that bullshit drama I created could have been avoided if I only trusted the people that loved me the most. It was such a relief that I didn't have to hide this secret that had been eating away at me for all these years. It's out in the open. I'm out. I'm Gay. And it's no big deal!

I didn't know anything about gay culture, and I didn't have any gay friends. The Victorian Aids Council had a support group called 'Young and Gay' which later I found out people called this 'Gay School'. During these sessions that were held once a week for six weeks we would talk about coming out, safe sex, the gay scene culture, bar, clubs, sex saunas and anything else we wanted to know. We had two guys facilitating the group their names were Todd and Gary. When I first laid my eyes on Todd, I had an instant crush.

Todd was about my height, short brown hair and a fit body. After the six weeks were over, we went to the Exchange Bar as a celebration for completing the course. After a few drinks, I got the courage to tell Todd that I thought he was hot, and I wanted him. Todd laughed it off, and I thought well that was a bust! But after a few hours of talking Todd pulled me aside and said, 'I'll kiss ya, but not here wanna come back to my house?' Hell yeah! I thought to myself. We left without saying goodbye to any of the others, jumped in a cab and went to Todd's apartment in Southbank, which was 15 mins from the city centre of Melbourne.

So, yes, we had sex. Todd was a top, and I had my first lesson on being a bottom. The next day we decided it's probably best to be mates. Todd became my best friend, and we hung out all the time. That's the thing about the gay culture, a lot of your close gay friends come out of having sex with the first, then realising that you're better off as friends than starting a romantic relationship.

Over the next year, it didn't take me long to fit right into the gay scene. Todd and I would be out most weekends, picking up guys, taking drugs and just having the time of our lives. I mean, that's what you do in your early twenties, isn't it? I took to the gay scene like a duck takes to water. But with my addictive personality, it didn't take long before I was doing drugs nearly every weekend, Ecstasy, Speed, MDA, GBH, Coke, Ketamine. Anything I was offered I took. I never did the real hard stuff like Heroin or injected Speed, I thought that was only for real drug junkies.

I started to get a reputation around the scene as a male slut! When I was eighteen and acting professionally, I had changed my last name from Bautista to Graham, my foster family's surname. So, my mates came up with a nickname they thought was hilarious 'Shane Graham fuck my arse!' No one really knew my history. Deep down, I started to become ashamed of my sexual disinhibitions while high, sleeping with different guys I would meet out on the weekends. I wanted to change, but I was addicted to the feeling of being wanted even if it was just for one night. The drugs I used as an escape as I tried to run from my past trauma as a child and my issues with abandonment, feeling worthless and not loving myself at all.

# CHAPTER 24

# ANDY

I first met Andy at The Imperial Hotel in Erskineville, southwest of Sydney's CBD which was featured in the 1994 Australian film Priscilla Queen of the Desert. Downstairs in the basement, the pub had a little nightclub, like an underground bar filled with people from the LGBTIQA+ community. In the middle of the crowd, I saw him, leaning against the wooden square pillar in the middle of the room watching the drag show.

For some reason, he stood out. He was a little taller than me, messy brown hair wearing a white t-shirt and blue jeans and his chest and arms bulged out of his t-shirt. I couldn't take my eyes off him. I was pissed and feeling confident enough to approach him even though I thought he was out of my league. Manoeuvring myself through the crowd to get to him, I tried not to spill my drink or get burnt by someone's cigarette. As I approached him, I stood next to him, looking forward while my heart was beating out of my chest. *Come on say, something dickhead!*

"Enjoying the show?" I asked.

"Sorry, what?" he didn't hear me.

"Enjoying the show?" I repeated a little louder and closer to his ear.

"Oh yeah, it's OK, you?" he asked.

"Yeah it's fun" I said.

After a slight pause, I leaned in closer and placed my left hand onto his waist.

"I'm Shane."

"Andrea, but my friends call me Andy" he replied with a grin.

"Sexy Italian man" I teased.

"I'm only half a sexy Italian man". Mum's English' he said jokingly.

"How old are you?" he asked.

"25, and I'm half Filipino and English" I answered

"Is your mum Filipino?" Andy asked.

"No, my dad is, and mum is English" I said.

"Nice mix" he smiled.

"Thanks" I shyly said.

"How old are you?" I asked.

"28. Am I too old for you?" He asked.

"Not at all, you're only a couple of years older than me" I laughed.

His brown eyes and smile were disarming, and for some reason, he felt familiar like we had met before, but I knew we hadn't. We chatted about me coming from Melbourne and why

I had moved up to Sydney, what he did for work, the usual small talk. His cologne smelled good. There's nothing that gets me going more than a guy's cologne, and when he looked into my eyes, it was like he could see into my soul.

I could feel the attraction between us. I hadn't realised that while we were talking, I had lent in towards him, our hips touching, and his hand was on my butt. My heart was pounding inside my chest as we talked loudly over the music into each other's ears. *I really want him to kiss me.* By this stage, the drag show had finished, and the DJ had started playing his set. I put on my flirty charm, laughing at all his jokes even when some weren't that funny, but I didn't care. I was in love at first sight. We stood there silent looking into other's eyes for only a moment, and I started to get self-conscious, so I giggled nervously.

"You're gonna be trouble" Andy said.

"Am I?" I asked

Andy smirked, and then it happened, what I was waiting for most of the night. He lent in and kissed me. His lips were tender and soft, as his tongue massaged mine, he pulled me in closer, holding me tight. At that moment, I felt safe and protected, feeling his strong arms around me. The music and everyone around us seemed to disappear as I put my hands up to the back of his T-shirt and rested them in the arch of his lower back.

Andy was such a great kisser. We seemed to have been kissing for hours, I didn't want to stop, but I needed to come up for air! I wanted to go home with him, but Andy said he had to get up early for work the next day. We swapped phone numbers, kissed a little more, then Andy left. My housemate Ryan, who I had moved up to Sydney from Melbourne with came up to me on the edge of the dance floor where I was standing with Andy.

"I saw you, you dirty slut! Who was he?" He was hot! Ryan piped.

"Andy" I said.

"Did you get his digits?" he asked.

I held up my phone and showed him Andy's number.

"Good for you, you bitch! Now help me find a man!"He demanded.

"I'm done. I think I'm gonna walk home" I said.

"Ok well, I'm staying then. Be safe!" he demanded.

We kissed each other on the cheek as I said goodbye and Ryan disappeared into the crowd. I had met Ryan in Melbourne seven months ago, working at one of the call centres in Melbourne. At the time, I was living with another gay couple, friends of mine I had met out on the gay scene. This was the time I was dating Ricco, remember him? The wog boy but that broke my heart after three months of dating.

The gay couple broke up but remained friends and asked me to move out so they could have separate bedrooms! *Typical gays!* I was just lucky enough that the timing was right, and Ryan was looking for a housemate at the time. We had gotten a two-bedroom spacious apartment in Kensington just out of the city. We had only been in the unit for six months before we received a "90-day notice to vacate letter" from the real estate as the owners wanted to move back in. We had been talking about how cool it would be to move to Sydney and how much of an adventure it would be. So that's what we did. And here we were.

I strolled down the main street of Erskineville, a suburb like Fitzroy in Melbourne. A fringe suburb with different occupants of people, the hippies, the arty, the homeless sleeping in between shop doors, streets filled with drunk people walking from pub to pub. I looked at my phone, and it was 2 am. I felt high as I walked down the street, smiling, and I couldn't get Andy out of my head, his kiss and his warm embrace. I felt on top of the world. As I pulled out a cigarette and lit it a man in his twenties ask me for a durry.

Usually, I would say no, but tonight I was feeling generous, so I handed him one and used my lighter to light it for him. He politely thanked me and ran up to his mates who walked ahead of him. Our apartment complex backed onto a side street 15-minute walk from the Imperial Hotel. Ryan and I secured a large two-bedroom apartment with a large lounge room and a balcony that wrapped around the side of the apartment, which overlooked the outside pool.

Our complex was a gated community that used to be the old Olympic Village during the year 2000 Olympics. I was happy to have reached our apartment, my legs and feet were sore from the walk, which was further than I expected. I undressed and fell into bed and felt the instant relief my legs and feet felt. I lay there wide-awake thinking of Andy. My hand ventured down inside my jocks, and I started pulling myself imagining Andy, making love to me.

*He kisses my neck as he runs his hands along my spine, feeling every inch of my back. We're in my room, and I'm lying naked on top of his naked body, caressing his muscular chest, and as we kiss, I feel the passionate fire that there is between us. He scoops me up into his muscular arms and flips me onto my back – I laugh. Andy kisses me again and then staring into my eyes, he lifts my legs over his shoulders and then enters me, slowly. He starts slow, kissing me, fucking me, making love to me.*

I start pulling myself-faster concentrating on achieving my orgasm imagining *Andy pounding me, faster and faster, it doesn't hurt he feels fantastic, he knows how to hit the spot. He starts to groan, and I can feel him shoot inside me, I can feel his throbbing cock, and his fluid is now inside me...*

Oh, shit, I'm coming! I think my come squirted onto my chest. There's a lot, it's been awhile. I reach below and grab my hand towel from the gym that was on the floor and wipe myself clean. I lay there in triumph, satisfied. Good night Andrea, the sexy Italian man. I hope you call me. I rolled over, closed my eyes and went to sleep.

# CHAPTER 25

# I'M A MISTRESS

When Andy told me, he had a boyfriend I'll be honest and say that I was disappointed, but it didn't stop me from pursuing him. These days, I'd like to think I have learnt some life lessons from my past mistakes and are more moral. But back then at the age of twenty-four, like most boys at that age and I say boys because I don't think at twenty-four, you're a grown man mentally; that we mostly thought with our dicks rather than our brains. Looking back, I know I did. I knew what I wanted and didn't let anything like a relationship get in the way. Selfish, I know and at the time, morally bankrupt, but I was in love, or was it lust that turned into love? That probably sounds more likely.

Andy and I had an attraction that was a magnetic force that drew us closer together, and with every hour we spent together, coupled with my seductive advances, the poor guy had no hope in being strong enough not to cheat on his boyfriend. Not having tickets on myself or anything, but unfortunately, I knew how to manipulate a person or situation to get what I wanted. This makes me sound evil but, in my defence, deep down I am a good person. I was just lonely and desperately searching for someone to love me; and like a drug, I was addicted to him.

I can't take all the blame; it wasn't like I held a gun to his head, and he had choices, and he chose to give in and have a friendship with me that mostly ended up in my bed. At the time, I complacently slept with Andy guilt free until the time I actually met his boyfriend, Josh. Then my guilt set in, but it didn't deter me, and I ended being the other woman. Josh was wary of me, and he had every right to be, but over time he warmed to me, treated me with kindness and that made my guilt even worse, but I couldn't stop.

At times Andy said we needed to just hang out as friends, and we tried this for a while however it never lasted long. I tried so hard to just be friends even to the point when I started seeing other guys, which I could because I was single. Andy would get jealous and hated the thought of another guy touching me, but I would remind him that he was the one in the relationship - that would never go down well.

It was a Wednesday night and Ryan and I went to mailbox night at the Stonewall Hotel, Sydney's gay bar up the top of the gay strip on Oxford St Darlinghurst. Mailbox night was a fun night for gay singles to meet other guys, and there was no shortage of talent. When you arrive, you're given a number to stick on your shirt, and this collates to the mailbox that's inside the venue. There were all sorts of different type of guys there, twinks, otters, bears, and muscle queens. With my dancer-fit physique and being aged 24, I fell into the twink category. If you liked a guy you would write them a note and put it into their mailbox number and eagerly await them to check their box - it was exciting! That's how I met Clint, a thirty-year-old reporter from England who was working for a newspaper in Sydney. He had left me a note in my mailbox saying, "meet me at the bar, I'm the guy with a bald head!"

I looked around and saw him standing at the bar watching me, and as our eyes locked, he smiled, holding up two drinks. He was very good looking, and I thought wow what confidence he has to assume I would have a drink with him. I loved his British accent and the way he carried himself, his sense of humour and charm. Did I go home with him? Of course, I did! I made sure Ryan was OK before I left. He was. I left him chatting to some guy.

"Be safe he said" as he kissed me on the cheek.

"You too" I replied.

Clint and I jumped in a taxi and went to his one-bedroom apartment in Darlinghurst. He must have gotten paid well as a reporter as his apartment was something out of a magazine. Floor to roof glass windows in his lounge room overlooking the city and other residences.

I didn't get to look around for long before he pushed me up against the wall and started kissing me. He was a good kisser! We ripped each other's t-shirts off, and he started kissing my neck, making his way down to my nipples. He was showing me his experience in the art of sex, knowing where all the erogenous zones were. I don't know if he was just drunk, horny or both, but he was eager and rough at the same time; something I hadn't experienced before, but I didn't mind.

We made love on his shaggy rug on the lounge room floor, cliché I know. We lay there sweaty and exhausted, and he held me in his arms while we kissed and chatted about life. We had a shower before climbing into his large king size bed, which I had noticed when I first entered his lavish apartment. He was so tender. Washing my back and kissing my shoulders, running his hand down my back until he reached between my buttocks.

With a hand full of soap, he washed between my butt cheeks, then started to play with my arsehole while kissing me from behind. Then Clint did something I had never experienced before. He knelt on his knees and spread my butt cheeks apart. When I felt his tongue licked my arsehole, I jumped and nearly hit my head against the shower wall. It felt strange at first, but when he kept going, it started feeling good. It is called 'rimming', and if you look up the meaning in the urban dictionary you will find:

> *Rimming - The act of using one's tongue*
> *on the anal rim of another person to gain*
> *and/or give sexual pleasure.*


And a pleasure it was! It got me so sexually aroused that I started begging for him to fuck me again. So, we went for round two in his shower. After getting clean again and drying ourselves off with his Egyptian cotton towels, we climbed into his king-sized bed. His bed was so comfortable it was like sleeping on a cloud, and for that night, I felt loved and protected as he held me all night, and I thought *I could get used to this.*

The smell of bacon, eggs and fresh coffee woke me up that Thursday morning. Clint came into the room and kissed good morning, I was worried about my morning breath, but Clint said I tasted just fine. As we lay in bed together, he said;

"Did you sleep well?"

"Yes, your bed is like a cloud" I smiled.

"Yeah, I love this bed. I made us breakfast, hope you're hungry?" Clint said.

"I can smell it, it smells amazing" I replied.

"Well let's eat I'm starving! It's the workout you gave me last night" Clint said with a cheeky grin. He looked so adorable.

"Oh, if you're cold you can wear my hoodie" Clint said, pointing to his red hoodie on the armchair in his room. Last night, I hadn't brought a jumper as the weather in Sydney always felt like it was in the mid-twenties, plus I hadn't expected to go home with anyone either.

"Thanks" I replied.

Just like in the movies, I was like the girl that walked out of the bedroom only wearing the guy's jumper and my under-wear. It had turned out that Clint and I had the day off work, so I could take my time and enjoy breakfast with this handsome stranger and not have to rush off and do the walk of shame -well not just yet. So, now I had a conundrum, I had feelings for two guys, Andy had a boyfriend, and Clint was single but not wanting to rush into anything serious -*What's a girl to do?*

I had been juggling two guys for the next two months. When Andy was with his boyfriend, I would see Clint, and when Clint was busy, I would see Andy. The best of both worlds! Clint was great sex, but the connection wasn't as secure as it was with Andy. When Andy would make love to me, it would feel like our bodies would become one. But after a while with Clint, it was just great sex. Clint became busy with work, and he made it clear to me that he wasn't looking for a relationship. I usually would have taken this hard, but my heart belonged to Andy.

The more I spend with Andy, the more I was falling in love with him. I believed Andy was my soul mate and that we were connected. Andy wasn't getting much connection from his boyfriend who was always working, and they hadn't taken the next steps in moving in together. There were times I would feel guilty that I was potentially destroying a two-year relationship, but I loved Andy, and it was easy to pretend that Andy belonged to me and that his boyfriend didn't exist. Andy and I would spend the weekends taking drugs, going clubbing and fucking. I must have been a terrible person back then because when I met his boyfriend, I didn't feel any remorse. I was selfishly thinking; *I wish Andy would leave him and be with me.*

After staying out all night clubbing Andy and I were still high, and we ended up lying in the morning sun at Centennial Park on Oxford street. Andy held me while I laid my head on his chest as we looked up at the morning sun shining through the trees and warming our bodies with the gentle breeze. Andy's big muscly arms were wrapped around my body like a warm, strong doona, and if I had a wish, I would wish that Andy could see that we were meant to be together. At that moment, I felt content.

I loved him so much, and when I thought about it, I started to become overcome with sadness. Maybe the drugs were beginning to wear off, but I realised that this wasn't real, and when the day was over, I would go home alone, and Andy would still be with his boyfriend.

*Holy shit I'm a mistress!*

# CHAPTER 26

# SECRETS OF A RENT BOY

I was first introduced to Ice by Sam, a blonde, blue-eyed guy that I met when I started working as a 'rent boy' in a brothel called 'Pleasure House' in the back streets of Darlinghurst. Pleasure House was the most famous gay and trannie brothel in Sydney. This wasn't my chosen profession; I fell into it out of need. I had a part-time job working for a music store in Chatswood NSW, a twenty-minute train ride over the Darling Harbor bridge. But, with my party lifestyle and addiction to drugs, I fell behind in my rent and needed to make some extra cash fast.

I had just finished a paid dancing gig at the after party for Sydney's Gay and Lesbian Mardi Gras held in Fox Studios. Tina Arena, Darren

Hayes and Courtney Act performed that night, and I was in the closing dance number for the night. Andy had lent me his car to travel to rehearsals the week before, and I remember running late for the cast meeting, and I ran into the building, plonked my bag on the ground as I sat down behind a group of fellow cast members. My bag hit a guy next to me, and I turned to apologise. *Holy shit it's Darren Hayes!* I felt embarrassed and star-struck, but he was kind and just laughed it off. The dancing gig only paid $250, but it was more the status of being cast for such a high-profile event.

After that gig, I was struggling financially. My housemate Ryan suggested that I try being a rent boy on the weekends. When Ryan was eighteen, he used to work as a rent boy in Melbourne and made a lot of money 'You give it away for free, why not get paid' he said with a laugh. I thought about it and thought, *well, what have I got to lose?* I took the day off my day job that coming Friday to attend an interview at the brothel.

The entrance was behind an old factory building with stairs leading up to a metal door with a red light placed above it. As I entered the building, I noticed the leather reception desk right from the entrance and behind it the greeting room where you meet the clients to introduce yourself, have a quick chat and then they pick which boy they want to spend their time with.

I was nervous. I didn't know what to expect, and I felt a little shame as I thought of what Joan would think of me now. I couldn't believe that my life had come to this, but I only had myself to blame. I owed my dealer $200 for the speed and pills I got on tick from last weekend, and he wasn't a guy to mess around with, so I had no choice. I was greeted by a man with salt and pepper hair who looked like he was in his forties, well-built and really good looking. He reached out to shake my hand as he greeted me with a smile. *Those dimples, he's so hot!*

"Hi, I'm Matt. I'm the manager here, how are you?"

"I'm a little nervous, I'm Shane."

"Don't be nervous, first time doing this?" Matt asked.

"Yeah," I answered.

Matt showed me to one of the bedrooms, ushered me to sit on the chair and closed the door behind him.

"Welcome to Pleasure House" Matt said.

"Thanks" I shyly grinned.

Matt asked me questions about myself, age, dick size, sexual experiences if I was a bottom or a top or versatile. I told him I was twenty-three years old, have had some sexual experience and that I was a bottom. I wasn't expecting that I would have to audition! I didn't know if this was a normal part of the interview or if Mark just liked hooking up with his new boys? But I didn't know any better and really needed to make more money, so I went along with it.

"Well I guess I better try you out" Matt said with a grin.

"Oh, OK", I said a little shocked, but I didn't mind as I had a slight attraction to him.

I walked over to where he was sitting and started kissing him, his hands felt all over my body, moving towards my arse as if he was studying it to see if it met his standards. He undid my jeans and pulled them down together with my underpants and squeezed my butt cheeks and said, "Nice arse, you'll do well here". He started to go down on me, and I remember thinking *if this is all I have to do, then it will be easy.*

"Suck me" he ordered as he pushed my head down towards his crotch. I obeyed and knelt down in front of him and unzipped his jeans and pulled his cock out. After we had finished, he said, "You're hired! You've got some talent kid."

Matt showed me around the brothel, explained how things worked and the rules such as;

1. Your clients must shower before you start.

2. Pull the bed cover off the bed and just change the sheets, we only dry clean the bed covers monthly so don't get cum on them, they're just there for decoration.

3. Put fresh towels in the bathroom after each booking and put the dirty sheets and towels in the laundry to be washed.

4. Condoms and lube are in the baskets beside the bed, and you'll find more supplies in the storeroom cupboard.

5. During the greetings, you are not allowed to show off your muscles by taking your top off and never show your cock as we aim to be fair amongst all you boys.

6. Never ever accept dates from clients!

7. Always try to extend the booking as it benefits you and the brothel, make the clients feel welcome, at ease and try not to let them cum, then they're more likely to extend for another hour.

8. No fucking between workmates, I don't care what you guys get up to outside of work hours, just not here.

"When you get an outcall, I'll explain how that works when the time comes, any questions?"

I felt so overwhelmed, but I didn't let Matt see that. I just smiled and shook my head *No*.

"Oh, best not to tell anyone your real name here, everyone has fake ones. Have thought of what you would call yourself?" Matt asked.

"No, I haven't" I said.

He looked at me intently as he thought of a name for me.

"I think you look like an Israel" he said.

"OK cool" I replied.

Matt introduced me to some of the other guys. They were sitting in a large room, some sleeping, eating, watching TV on the couch. There were a couple of transvestites doing their nails, and as I walked into the room with Matt, one of them smiled.

"Fresh meat boys" she laughed.

She was tall with burgundy hair and a slim body with large breasts and legs for days. She seemed excited to see a new face because she enthusiastically jumped out of her seat to shake my hand.

"I'm Tiffany" she screeched.

"Hi, I'm Israel".

Tiffany eagerly introduced me to the others pointing at each guy with her long red acrylic fingernails.

"That's Brad and Trent sitting on the couch watching TV, Blake sleeping on the bunk, Seb our ex-Czech military porn star and Sam sitting behind you."

The guys all waved and said hi and started asking me the normal getting to know you questions. Which suburb did I live? Wass this my first time? What brought me here? Everyone was inquisitive about the new guy.

"If you're up for it a lot of my regulars like doubles" Sam said.

"Doubles?"

"You know, two of us, a threesome."

"Oh, cool yeah that sounds like fun."

"Aww, I get to break in the newbie."

Everyone laughed, I wasn't sure how to take Sam at first, but we ended up being work friends. Sam was kind, taking me under his wing and showing me the tricks of the trade. He was gorgeous, blond messy hair, blue eyes, muscular build, large cock, tight bubble butt, five years experience and versatile, the complete package. Sam was only twenty-five but still looked like an eighteen-year-old. Everyone was attractive. Seb and Sam were the muscular jocks, Brad was the stocky hairy cub, and Trent was the young, thin twink.

With all these hot guys to compete with I thought I had no shot of getting work, however, the men that walked through the door had different sexual fantasies and desires. I was shocked when a lot of straight tradies came into the brothel after a Friday night at the pub with mates, fulfilling their secret sexual desires. Tiffany did very well with the straight guys that liked 'trannies.' She joked about how they loved getting fucked by a chick with a dick. Other men were shy, lonely or stuck in a heterosexual marriage and felt they had too much to lose to come out as gay. Whatever the client's reasons were their own, who was to judge. My job was to fulfil their sexual desire. Sex exchanged for money and money exchanged for sex.

This was the new world I had entered into, and in the beginning, it was exciting. My first weekend, I brought home $1500 cash and was able to pay my overdue rent and keep up my drug habit and party lifestyle. Being a rent boy started to become addictive. The money was good, having sex with strange men was empowering and exhilarating. I just loved sex. Deep down, the clients were fulfilling my desires of feeling wanted and loved and I was fulfilling their sexual fantasies. And the guys and Tiffany were fun to hang out with, they really made me feel like part of the family.

I had already been at the brothel for three weeks, and the nervous, scared newbie had turned into a seasoned pro. It felt good to walk in confident and sure of myself and my sexual abilities. It was a quiet Saturday night, and I had only had one booking for that last five hours. The night started to pick up a little by 12am, but I was the destitute prostitute who couldn't get a booking no matter how charming I was in the introductions.

It just wasn't my night. Sam seemed to be getting a lot of the bookings, which pissed the other guys off. Sam was sensitive to this and tried not to rub it in anyone's faces. Sam and I became close, and he always tried to look out for me. He knew I was having a shit night, so being the friend, he was, he talked his next client into having a double. Sam came into the staff room and grabbed my hand,

"Get up you poor slag I have a surprise for you!"

"A double?"

"Yeah, baby!"

"Oh fun, you're the best Sammy!"

The client's name was Hendrick, a thirty-five-year-old tradie from the northern parts of Sydney. Hendrick was a tall, handsome tradie. He wasn't ripped but had the rugby player build. He was bisexual but being a wog boy, he kept it hidden from his family and mates. Hendrick had a girlfriend who was a flight attendant, and whenever she was away for work, he would visit Sam to get his dose of cock and arse. We were in the deluxe room, which had a spa and a kings size bed, and the room was designed like an expensive hotel room. Hendrick was showered and ready to go.

Hendrick had brought in a bag of cocaine, and we did lines on the side of the spa and drank Champagne. He loved to see two guys together, so Sam and I put on a show for him, while Hendrick pulled himself. After finishing in the spa, we moved onto the king-sized bed. Hendrick laid on the bed and pulled me onto his cock while Sam sat on his face.

Hendrick must have secretly jacked off to a lot of gay porn because he acted like a porn star, throwing Sam and me around the bed while he took it in turns in fucking us. I had never had so much fun in my life and sex, while high, was euphoric. The session lasted for three hours, and we both got an excellent cut each which, made up for the shitty night.

"I'll always look after you, babes."

"Thanks, Sam, that was so much fun! I'll return the favour."

"Damn straight, you will. Now help me fix this room up, bitch!"

I helped Sam get the room ready for the next booking, and we giggled like schoolgirls as we stumbled around the room still high from the copious amounts of coke we had snorted. We finished our shift at 3:30am, Sunday morning. Matt would hand us the money we made that night, and I would have to catch a fifteen-minute taxi ride back to my apartment in Erskineville.

Sam was complaining as the coke was wearing off and wanted to kick on. He asked me back to his apartment to hang out and unwind. I had no plans, so I accepted his invitation. Sam invited Seb to come with us, so the three of us walked back to Sam's apartment, which was only a ten-minute walk from 'Pleasure

House'. Sam led us into his bedroom, and he went to his bedside drawer and pulled a glass pipe and a small plastic bag of what looked like tiny white crystals. I had heard of crystal meth, ice, shard and shabu before but I had never smoked it. Sam went first then passed the pipe to Seb and Seb then gave it to me. We sat on Sam's bed chatting about our previous shift at Pleasure House and some of the weird Jon's that we had encountered.

It didn't take long before the effects of ice took hold. I felt invincible, confident, clear-headed, an increase in energy and horny as hell. Sam and Seb started making out and taking each other's t-shirts off, and I began to get really aroused watching these two hot guys together. Sam turned to me and kissed me, ripping off my t-shirt while Seb started sucking my nipple. It was euphoric, every sensation was heightened by this drug I had never tried before but loved for the first time. Sam laid down on the bed, and I started to suck him while Seb began to fuck me. We all came a few times without resting in between and took turns sucking and fucking each other, only stopping to have another hit.

We were at it for around six hours before we became exhausted. I was in love with ice, it made you feel like you had a superpower, a confidence and sex drive that no other drug had given me before. Every shift at Pleasure House I couldn't work without a smoke, my performance in the bedroom improved and my body became more defined as I lacked the appetite to eat much food.

The comedowns were a bitch, though, and I became irritable, had difficulty sleeping, had headaches and dizziness. I went to my doctor and got a prescription for Valium, and these helped counteract the comedowns and give me some sleep. I took a few sickies from the music store during the week to recover, and once Friday night came along, I would do it all again. This cycle repeated itself for the two months while I worked as a rent boy, but the euphoric feelings of getting high on the weekends outweighed the comedowns during the week.

I started to have more sick days off from the music store, exhausting all the paid sick days, and now when I called in sick, I wasn't getting paid. I didn't give a shit 'cos I was earning between $1000-$1500 a weekend. After I paid rent and bills, food was an afterthought and drugs were my number one priority, I was hardly hungry anyway. I would eat maybe once or twice a day. Ice would reduce your appetite, and I was continually losing weight, which was great because I looked more ripped. Having the dancers ripped body with my smooth olive skin was a real attraction to the men that came in looking for a boy to fulfil their fantasies.

# CHAPTER 27

# IN TOO DEEP NOW

Andy had called me on a Saturday afternoon when I was about to start my shift at Pleasure House. He wasn't happy with my new weekend job; it was like he didn't like the thought of guys touching me, as if I belonged to him.

"Why are you doing this?"

"I needed the money, and it's kinda fun, Andy."

"Well, I don't want random guys fucking you!"

"It's got nothing to do with you! You're not my boyfriend, are you?"

"So, you're doing this to get back at me?"

"No, Andy, I'm not! But yes, you broke my heart. You promised me something that you knew you couldn't follow through with and I believed you!"

"I'm sorry, Shane, hurting you wasn't my intention. I do love you. You can just quit, come over to mine now, just quit."

Andy's offer was tempting. I was still in love with him, but I knew he wouldn't leave his boyfriend. He rejected me, and I still carried that hurt around with me and being a working boy was a good distraction from the pain I was feeling. When Andy didn't choose me, it was like a kick in the guts that I would carry around with me for a long time. And I lied to him, I was angry with him. I loved him, and I hated him at the same time. I would have given anything to have him hold me in his arms, kiss me and make love to me like he once did, but I would just end up at the same place I am now.

"I can't, it hurts too much."

"Please don't do this, Shane"

"Andy, I'll talk to you later, I've gotta go."

As I hung up the phone, I burst into tears, I could feel the heartache of what we once had, but it was over. Then suddenly I just stopped. I wiped my eyes with the sleeve of my jumper. *Get your shit together, Shane!* I walked up to the stairs, and when I reached inside the building, I made a beeline for the toilets and washed my face. Andy did break my heart, but somehow, this job made me harden my heart so no one could break it again.

I had been at Pleasure House for almost two months now, I was comfortable, I was a part of the crew. Having an addictive personality, I guess I was addicted to the sex, instant gratification, feeling wanted and desired, my new friendships I had made with the other boys, the drugs and of course the money. I was hooked, and I didn't want to give this up for anybody, not even Andy.

I saw Matt showing a new boy around the brothel. I just smiled to myself because not long ago I was the newbie, the fresh meat, but now I was a seasoned prostitute. Since the threesome with Seb and Sam, my taste for ice increased, and I started buying a couple of points off Sam every weekend, so I could do double shifts to earn more money.

Then it began to become twice a week to get through the day, smoking in the morning to have more energy at my day job at the music store. On the Sundays, the brothel closed at 2am which was earlier than the weeknights and Saturday nights, which closed at 4am, so some of us would go party at Arc Bar in Darlinghurst, the most prominent gay club in Sydney.

Being a rent boy was now my only source of income. The music stores area manager Dave came into my store I was managing and caught me out the back storeroom smoking a point of ice behind the CD shelf. I was mortified that he found me and begged him to not fire me, but he fired me on the spot. I could tell he was disappointed in me, and I felt awful as he had trusted me and given me a chance to step up as a manager.

He was kind enough to maintain my dignity and let me go through the back door of the store, so I didn't have to face my staff members. I was high at the time, so the gravity of my situation had not dawned on me as yet. Fuck it, I earn more as a rent boy anyway, I thought.

I had a bad attitude. The 'world owes me mentality' reared its ugly head and having Borderline Personality and Detachment Disorder. I found it hard to regulate my emotions and thought processes. It didn't help to be under the influence of methamphetamines either as I couldn't give a shit about my life, I was angry at the universe for dealing me a shit life and mad that Andy didn't love me enough to leave his boyfriend for me.

Looking back at the situation I had found myself in, I wanted to hurt Andy by making him watch me go downhill, but the only person I was really hurting was myself. The following Friday night at Pleasure House, I was hanging in the lounge with Sam, Seb, Brad and Tiffany laughing at her stories of the weird things she got asked to do.

"This one guy wanted to lay in my lap while sucking my tit like a baby being breastfed while he jacked himself off! Sick fuck" she said disgustedly.

"Did you charge fantasy rates?" I asked.

"Damn right sweetheart, a whole $200 extra and the sick fuck paid it!"

We all burst out laughing as fantasy rates are only $50 bucks! This poor sucker got totally done. Matt walked into the room and called my name.

"Israel."

"Yeah?" I answered.

"You have an out call, get ready in ten minutes" Matt said.

James was our driver who took us to the out calls and acted as our personal bodyguard. James was in his late forties, had been a bodybuilder in his twenties and managed to maintain his muscular look. He had tatts down his arms and looked like a guy you didn't want to mess with. James gave me a crash course on what to do on an outcall.

> *When you greet the receptionist say you're here to meet your friend (insert name here.) When the 'Jon' answers the door and lets you into his hotel room, you*

*OK, I can do this* I said to myself. Outcalls pose a lot of risks as you didn't have Matt to vet them first and you didn't know who or what you were walking into. James pulled the car over in front of one of Sydney's elite hotels, and I turned to James in disbelief

"You're shitting me!"

James smiled, "Go make some money, kid."

I kissed James on the cheek "Thanks" and left his car and walked towards the hotel. I felt out of place here, I would never in my wildest dreams be able to afford to stay here. Marbled floors with large crystal chandeliers hanging from the roof and brass railings that lead you up to the staircase to the hotel lobby. As I walked towards the reception desk there was a lady in her forties, blonde hair pulled back into a tight bun dressed in a grey pantsuit, she looked really posh.

"Hello, can I help you?"

"Yeah, I'm Sha…Israel, I'm here to see my friend Simon in room 356" I nearly fucked up and gave her my real name, *idiot!*

"Sure, take the centre lift to floor 35" she said with a smile.

I thanked her, and as I walked towards the lifts, I could see my reflection, and I didn't like what I saw. I had lost more weight and looked like skin and bone. I knocked on 356, and a medium built Asian man in his late twenties answered the door with nothing on but the white hotel towel wrapped around his waist.

"Hi handsome I'm Israel."

"Hi, I'm Joseph."

Joseph let me into the room, he seemed nervous.

"This is my first time I'm a little nervous' he confessed.

I reassured him that I would take good care of him and all he had to do is relax and enjoy himself. Joseph handed me a wad of cash in 100 dollar bills, I counted it, yep $400 there for the hour. I called James and said everything was fine. I put the cash in my satchel bag and asked if I could freshen up in the bathroom. I needed a fix, so I could perform. I was tired and needed that extra boost of energy.

I sat on the toilet, and I got my crack pipe out of my bag and used my house key to scoop a little crystal out of my small plastic baggie and tapped them into the bulb of the pipe. I placed my lighter under the glass bulb and heated up the Ice and sucked back on what I can only describe as heaven.

I came out of the bathroom, ready and raring to go. Joseph was lying back on the bed, already dressed for the occasion. I started sucking his cock, but nothing was happening no matter what I tried, I just couldn't get that sucker to get hard. Embarrassed, Joseph said, 'It's not you, I'm just exhausted. Can you just massage me naked?'

"Sure thing."

So, he rolled over onto his front, and I massaged him using the hotel's massage oil for the rest of the hour. *Easiest money I've had to make.* Joseph was kind and sweet. He worked in finance and was from Perth, in Sydney for business.

He identified as straight, however, was always curious about what it was like to be with a guy. Halfway through his massage, I turned him over, and there was his hard cock standing to attention like a faithful soilder ready for battle. I climbed onto him and sat on it. It only took him less than five minutes before he came, and the hour was up. I felt like I just completed a community service. I helped a man feel satisfaction, triumphant in his efforts, although I did most of the work. Another satisfied customer. From here on my confidence grew and I was determan to be the best rent boy I could be.

# CHAPTER 28

# IN TROUBLE

I was spending around $100 every three days on meth and $300 during our nights out on booze and pills, K, speed, whatever was on offer to escape my life. During the week meth became my morning pick me up, like coffee and on the weekend, it got me through the weekend as I worked double shifts on a Saturday and Sunday at Pleasure House. Uppers got me through the day and night and downers helped me sleep. This turned into a constant cycle that I couldn't break out of, and even if I wanted to, I probably wouldn't want to try.

Andy and I were hardly speaking, and I missed the warmth of his arms when he used to hold me in bed after making love. As a rent boy, you have different experiences with different men. I felt sorry for the married men that had to pay for what they could get for free if they were brave enough to come out and live the life they wanted.

I thought about that assumption I was making so I decided to ask. Jason was a thirty-five-year-old bisexual guy happily married to his wife for five years and had two young kids. She knew about his sexual orientation and was happy with it as long as he wore protection and used a professional service. I was surprised, not all married men are in the closet.

Jason was a lawyer. I didn't know what law he practised, and I didn't really ask. Jason wasn't into the small talk, he just wanted to get straight to business. As a lawyer and family man as he was time poor. Jason would book me for an hour every Friday at 6pm on his way home. He was very attentive to my body, and it was like I was the client, and he was the pro. What got him off the most was being in charge and making me feel pleasure. The hour would go by so fast, and I wish I could have spent the night with him.

I would think how lucky his wife was to be able to receive his attentiveness, Jason's sensuality, his eagerness to please, then waking up in his arms every morning. I longed for that connection, I used to get that from Andy on the nights we spent together. I missed him, but I was too proud to go back to him because sleeping with random men for money was a lot easier, I could turn my feelings off which was better than the emotional turmoil I felt with Andy.

Like any honeymoon phase where it's fun, exciting and exhilarating living a double life, now I'd lost my day job at the music store I had to pick up a few more shifts during the weeknights to afford my living costs and drug habit; after a while, it became the same old routine. Intro, get booked, service the guy, shower, clean the room, then wait for the next booking, repeat. You don't get to choose the clients that book you, sometimes you're lucky enough to get the hot tradie types but other times you get the lonely old men, fat men and ugly men. The appeal was wearing thin, and I wasn't enjoying this work as much anymore, but the money was too hard to turn away from.

I was a pro with outcalls, and the work was plentiful as there was only a couple of us that would do them. Outcalls paid the most, and I would go out at least five times over the weekend. Matt told me that this guy was an out of towner, so if he seems sketchy, call Jason. I went on the call, and as Jason and I approached the hotel, it wasn't the flashy hotels I was used to; this one was a budget hotel, and I was a little apprehensive. I knocked on the door, and I heard a husky voice.

"Come in."

I entered the darkened room and saw a large figure sprawled over the bed.

"Hi I'm Israel"

"Hey, money is on the bench."

"Ok thanks. Can I please use your phone?"

"Sure, it's in front of you."

I called in to report that things were OK, and I had the money.

"Get your butt over here" he demanded.

"What's your name, honey?" I asked.

"Names aren't important, now take off your clothes" he ordered.

I felt uneasy, he smelt like beer and cigarettes, it was apparent he was drunk, and I should have called Jason and ended the booking, but I needed the cash. He pulled me on top of him and started to rub his little prick between my arse cheeks. Then he flipped me over, and his fat body was crushing me. He kissed me and shoved his tongue so far down my throat that I nearly gagged. He tried to put it inside me, but I stopped him.

"Safety first mate" I said, handing him a condom.

He protested, but I told him that he couldn't fuck me without a condom. After grumbling, he complied. His little dick darted in and out of me, and it hurt. He put on an act that he was the most fantastic lover, when in fact he was totally rubbish. I couldn't wait for the hour to be over. The alarm on my phone and time was up, he came and seemed satisfied. I couldn't wait to get back to the brothel and shower. As I was getting dressed, he asked to extend, and I politely said no. I told him that I had more bookings back at the brothel. He became aggressive, trying to grab my arm, stopping me from leaving.

"Mate, let go of me!" I demanded.

His grip became stronger, hurting me, and I started to panic. He started yelling.

"I give a lot of money to your boss, and I call the shots! You fucking whores think you're so better than me!"

He pushed me onto the bed, face down, holding me down with his weight. I tried to get out from under him, but he was too heavy. He started to pull my jeans down, spreading my legs while pushing my head down further into the mattress with one hand.

"Get the fuck off me!" I screamed.

"I'm gonna fucking breed you like the little bitch you are."

"Please stop!" I pleaded.

But he didn't stop. As he attempted to enter me, I heard a loud crash at the front door. Just like a knight and shining armour, Jason came bursting through the door. Jason always said if I were late coming out after the booking, he would come looking for me.

"Get off him, or I will fucking drop you!" Jason screamed.

Jason pulled the fat guy off me and punched him in the face, and he fell to the ground. I was shaking, I scrambled up towards the head of the bed, pulling up my jeans. I walked over the fat guy who just tried to rape me and booted him once in the head and his fat guts as I yelled.

"Fuck you! You fat piece of shit!"

Jason grabbed me and walked out of the room. As we were heading towards the car, the fat guy, still lying naked on the floor started screaming, "You'll fucking regret this!"

"Are you OK?" Jason asked.

"Thank god you came in when you did, that fat prick!"

Jason picked me up into his arms as I held onto his shoulders. I leaned into his muscular chest. Exhausted but relieved I was now safe. At that moment, Jason was 'The Bodyguard', and I was Whitney!

When we arrived back, I headed straight for the showers. I couldn't wait to scrub off that fat arse stench off me. As I replayed what just happened in my head, I burst into tears. I realised that I was moments away from being raped. As I was getting dried and dressed, Matt came into the room furiously. He asked if I was ok and apologised for sending me out there.

"He's never done this before. I'm really sorry". Matt hugged me, and I felt safe again. Matt told me to call it a night.

"Go home, Jason will drive you. Are you sure you're OK?" Matt asked, concerned.

"I'll be ok. Just need some rest" I said.

I got my stuff out of my locker and shoved the contents into my bag and left, not saying goodbye to the others. I didn't want to have to rehash everything, I just needed to get the fuck out of there. Jason drove me home, and I went straight to my room. I put on my PJ's and crawled into bed.

My heart was racing, and my thoughts were running a million miles inside my head. I needed to sleep. I hadn't slept since Friday night, and now it was Saturday at 10pm. I still had some Valium left from the last prescription I got from my GP. I popped out three tablets from the packet and downed them with some water from my water bottle beside my bed and eventually fell asleep.

# CHAPTER 29

# REALITY CHECK

It was Saturday morning, and I woke up feeling like shit. I was still drowsy from the Valium I took. Usually, the maximum dose is 10mg, but in taking three tablets, I had taken 15mgs. I had a higher tolerance to drugs these days, so I had to take more than the prescribed amount to be able to feel the same result. It was a cold, wintery day, and I couldn't face another night at the brothel. I needed a break to recover.

I texted Andy to see what he was doing. My housemate Ryan was out for the day, and I was home alone. I needed some comfort. I needed Andy. Andy messaged back and said he could come over in an hour, so I had time to have a shower and get myself together. I stood under the hot water of the shower for thirty minutes as the water pressure massaged by sore back from the night before.

Suddenly, I was hit with a wave of emotions and burst into tears as last night came flooding back to me, *I was nearly raped.* I felt like I had hit rock bottom, and I was another state away from Tom, Marie, Kate and Lilly, my second family in Melbourne. I missed them all and couldn't believe the trouble I had gotten myself into.

The intercom buzzed and on the screen was Andy's handsome face. I missed that face. I hadn't seen it for four months. I buzzed him up and waited for him to knock on my front door. I was feeling nervous and excited at the same time to see him. As I opened the door and saw him standing there, I burst into tears and fell into his arms. I was shaking, holding him tight and feeling his arms around me had reminded me of how warm and safe he felt.

"I'm sorry bub" I sobbed.

Andy picked me up and carried me to my room, laying me on my bed. He lay beside me, and I curled up into his embrace. At first, I was scared to tell him what had happened last night as I thought he would get angry with me. Andy went to massage the back of my neck, and I winced. When he saw the bruises, he knew something had gone down last night.

"What the fuck happened?" Andy asked.

I told him that I was nearly raped by a 'Jon' during an outcall and he lost his shit.

"I'll fucking kill him! Where does he live?"

"He was an out of towner. He will be long gone by now."

Andy placed his hands around my face so I would pay attention to what he was about to say.

"You need to quit!"

"I know, I know. I'm stuck. Who's gonna hire an ex-rent boy?"

"You don't have to put that on your resume you know" Andy laughed.

"I really need a point right now", I said.

"No! Ice? Really babe? Party drugs are one thing, but you don't need that shit!"

I nodded in agreement. I knew deep inside that I needed to stop, but I didn't know where to get help. Andy suggested the LGBTI sexual health clinic in Kings Cross. I promised Andy I would go and seek advice.

Andy never left the house without putting on his cologne. He always wore Calvin Klein and, damn, he smelled good! Andy was my kryptonite, and I was his. I nuzzled my nose into his neck and sniffed him, deeply. "You smell so good" I said. Andy kissed the bruises on my neck as if to take away the pain. His soft kisses dulled the hurt. With the sound of the rain gently pattering against the window, Andy made love to me. I was so happy to be in his arms again, to feel his sensual touch, his kiss and the warmth of him inside me.

That afternoon I momentarily forgot he had a boyfriend and pretended that he was mine and I would have him for the rest of my life. It was like we were in sync. When we came at the same time, and at that moment, I felt he was my soul mate. Then reality set in. As we lay there staring up at the ceiling, I knew that I would always be second best, Andy's mistress, and I deserved better. Andy had no intention of leaving his boyfriend for me. The truth sometimes hurts, but I knew that I had to get into reality. I was so in love with him, but I needed to end this.

The next day I called Tom he knew straight away something was wrong, he could hear it in the tone of my voice.

"I'm in trouble!" I said.

"What's happened, mate?"

I filled him in my life for the last six months and how I hadn't achieved my dancing goals and instead got addicted to ice and became a male escort. He was shocked.

"You need to come home right now!"

I began to cry, hearing Tom's voice. He gave me some reassurance and made me realise that the real people that cared for me were all in Melbourne. I told Ryan that I was going back to Melbourne. He was sad but understood. It only took him a few days to find another roommate to take my room. I went to the bulk billing GP clinic and told the doctor of my ice use and that I wanted to stop but didn't want to go into hospital. He gave me pamphlets on ice addiction and how to withdraw safely.

"It's going to be hard on your own. I can't convince you to withdraw at the hospital?" he said, checking if I would change my mind.

"No, I'm moving back to Melbourne in two days. I'm going to detox at my brothers". I said.

The doctor prescribed me with fifty Valium tablets to help with the withdrawal and cravings. I borrowed Ryan's care and drove over to Andy's. He could see something was wrong as soon as he saw my face. My heart was beating so fast. How was I going to tell him I'm moving back to Melbourne?

"Andy, I'm leaving. Going back to Melbourne."

"Wait, What? Why?" he said, confused.

"I'm sick, and I can't do this, us, anymore. It hurts too much because I'm so in love with you!"

Andy stood there in silence, looking at me. He knew we liked each other and that we enjoyed having fun together, but he never thought I was in love with him.

"You're never going to leave him" I said.

Andy looked to the ground, defeated.

"I can't. I love him still."

"And me?" I asked him.

"I love you too but..."

"You're not in love *with* me" I said, finishing his sentence.

Andy sat on the arm of his couch and burst into tears with his head in his hands. I felt my heart sink. He looked so vulnerable, and I felt sorry for him, hated seeing him cry. I walked over to him, and he wrapped his arms around my waist. I leant down and hugged him as we both cried realising this was going to be goodbye for good.

The next day Ryan had driven me to the airport, and I was on the plane back to Melbourne. Heartbroken and withdrawing from ice, I felt sick and had a massive headache. I took a couple of the Valium the doctor gave me with some Panadol and fell asleep until the plane touched down in Melbourne. Walking through the terminal, I switched my mobile back on, and there was an SMS from Andy.

> *"I'm sorry for hurting you. I hope you arrived back in Melbourne safe – Love Andy".*

I replied:

> *"Just arrived in Melbourne. I fell for you, but I guess I wasn't good enough for you to choose me."*

Andy didn't reply back, and that is the last time I heard from him.

# CHAPTER 30

# GETTING CLEAN

I spent a week mostly sleeping in the spare bedroom at Tom and Marie's three-bedroom apartment detoxing of ice. The first few days were hell on earth. I had the chills, was always sweaty, I couldn't sleep at night no matter how hard I would try. I had a dry mouth and couldn't quench my thirst, no matter how much I drank. The headaches were so bad that it felt like my brain was exploding inside my skull, and no amount of paracetamol could completely take the pain away.

As my body craved for a smoke of a point of ice. I became irritable and couldn't sit still. Tom and Marie started to get really worried about me, so they took me to the doctor who prescribed Valium again to help me with the withdrawals and help me sleep. As the days went by, the withdrawals lessened, and I started feeling normal again, just tired, so tired I slept for a week, only waking to eat, drink and use the toilet. I swore that after going through that detox period, I would never touch ice again. And I never did.

In my early twenties, I had a provisional diagnosis of Borderline Personality Disorder (BPD and a definite diagnosis of major depressive and anxiety disorder originating from my childhood trauma. BPD consists of extreme black and white thinking, chronic feelings of emptiness, instability in relationships, self-image, identity, and behaviour disturbances, often leading to self-harm and impulsivity.

To be honest, it was clear that I was suffering from this since I was fourteen years old, but I refused to see a psychologist.

Therefore, I wasn't diagnosed earlier on in my life. Looking back now, I can't believe I survived. I got through my young adult life unscathed, and I think to this day that my Nanna has been watching out for me, protecting me and making sure I was safe. Thanks, Nan!

I needed some time to recover before I was able to cope with full-time employment. I started receiving unemployment bene-fits from Centrelink, and I was exempt from looking for work for the next few months on mental health and drug addiction grounds. I never attended a detox rehabilitation centre because I was unaware of public services and thought that the only way to enter a rehabilitation centre was to pay a lot of money.

So, I just relied on the support of Tom and Marie. With the drugs out of my system, I could concentrate on what I needed to do next.

It was suggested through a job searching agency that I should take the time to study. My caseworker handed me a pamphlet on the 'New Enterprise Incentive Scheme' (NEIS). The NEIS program was a Government scheme to assist people who were unemployed to set up their own business. I had a bachelor's degree in graphic design, so I thought I could get back into graphic design and work for myself. I attended the full training time during the week at RMIT in Melbourne's CBD. At the end of the 26 weeks, I had a comprehensive business plan and a qualification in a Certificate 4 in Business Management.

The NEIS program was great, as the money I earnt in my business for the twelve months didn't get deducted from my unemployment benefits, plus, I had a business mentor that I would see every quarter. Another guy I did the course with, who I'll call Jack, was doing a signwriting business, so we paired up and rented a warehouse in Richmond and shared the rent.

Jack and I gave work to each other, which helped grow our businesses. At this point in time, I have been six months clean of drugs. I was proud of myself. I have achieved a goal, and this gave me the confidence to take charge of my life. My graphic design business was taking off within the first few months of opening. I had plenty of clients, and I was earning a living. I finally felt I was getting back on my feet.

Tom and Marie wanted to move closer to the city, so we moved to St Kilda East. I lived with them for another month until I saved enough money for the bond and first month's rent to move into my own apartment. I found a one-bedroom apartment in St Kilda about 10 minutes from Tom and Marie's.

I was enjoying working for myself, I had autonomy and was on the road to recovery. In the beginning, I was thriving in my business, but as time went on, I found it hard to compete with the larger design studios. I could have applied for a graphic design position at a design studio, but I lacked the confidence to be amongst younger, more talented designers than myself and the thought of the pressure design studios put on their designers to meet deadlines gave me high anxiety.

After my twelve months of being in the NEIS program was up, I was going to be on my own. The Centrelink payments that were helping me keep afloat were about to stop, and I knew that I would not survive financially if I continued with my graphic design business. So, I closed it down. The stress of running your own business was becoming too overwhelming and taxing on my mental health.

I didn't want to become unwell again, so I applied for a call centre job working for an outsourcing company that had a portfolio of companies like Telstra BigPond Internet, ANZ Bank and AGL Electricity. I got a position as a customer care service agent for Bigpond, and that is when I met my long-term friends, Ally, Dan and Monte.

It is often rare to keep in contact with work friends. However, Ally, Dan and Monte and I became a family. We have been friends for twelve years now and through the ups and the downs we have held each other up. I feel blessed every day to have such good friends in my life.

# CHAPTER 31

# GAMILY

I hadn't seen my cousin Tania much after high school. She had gotten married and had two young girls, and I, well, you know what I was doing.  The 2006 annual Melbourne Midsumma Festival was coming up, and I received a text message on my mobile phone from Tania.

"Hey Cuz, it's been a while. Would love to come to Midsumma with you! Let me know if you're going?" Tania.

"Hi, there! Great to hear from you! Yes, it's this Sunday, I'm going with my boyfriend and his friends. Come tag along it will be grand!" I replied.

I was pleasantly surprised, hearing from her. I had been thinking of reaching out the week before, because growing up we had always been close. Tania was still the responsible one out of all us kids. I was the reckless and defiant one. At this stage, I had a boyfriend named Chaz. I had met him through a friend of a friend at the Greyhound gay bar in St Kilda on a night out. The thing I most loved about him was his personality. He was a cool cat. Nothing much phased him. He always seemed calm, and it took a lot to make him angry. Chaz was just a fun-loving guy. But, like in all my disastrous relationships, this only lasted three months before I heard,

"I love you but… *I'm not in love with you.*"

And then it was over. I never learn my lesson. Every time I start dating a guy, I think he's the one and that he's the one I'll marry. But, within three months, I'm left devastated and humiliated because once again I just jump in giving my whole heart to another guy, who yet again breaks it. Tom's mobile was getting full of numbers of the guys I would date. I would introduce them, and he would start to be friends with them. Until after the three-month mark hit and I'd have to tell him 'Oh, we broke up, so we don't speak to him anymore.'

This became a running joke as Tom started to have more gay guys phone numbers in his phone than I did! So, Tom made up a rule that I wasn't allowed to introduce any guys I was dating until after three months. I was so excited all week and Sunday couldn't have come around fast enough. Being self-centred, I thought how awesome it was that Tania wanted to support me and be involved in my world, oblivious to the fact there could be another reason Tania was interested in Midsumma.

*Knock. Knock. Knock.*

I opened the front door, and there was my beautiful cousin standing in front of me. We gave each other the biggest hug, happy to see one another.

"Oh, my God! Come in. It's so good to see you" I shrieked.

"Want some wine? Red or White?" I asked.

"Ah...white, please" Tania answered.

As we were drinking our wine, I ask Tania:

"So, what made you interested in coming to Midsumma? How's Alan and the girls?"

Tania stares at me amused that I am so oblivious to the obvious.

"Um...Alan and I have separated. And why do you think I wanted to come today?" she answers.

I give her a blank look. I still have no fucking clue.

"Because I'm GAY! You dumb arse!" Tania says, laughing at me.

"What the Fuck? Oh, my God! Since when?" I asked.

"I had always had that feeling, you know, but was too afraid, to be honest with myself. I loved Alan, but after the girls were born, I knew I couldn't pretend anymore" Tania explained.

I was so proud of her bravery. To come out as gay, end her marriage and have to tell the Danish side of the family, especially Aunty Kerry, would have taken a lot of guts. The family at first were in shock and upset as they all loved Alan, but eventually came to accept that this is who Tania is. I was also so happy that I wasn't the only Gay in the Village! You can't help who you're sexually attracted to or love. Being gay is NOT a choice. I don't give a fuck what anyone says. When I hear that comment, it infuriates me, and I always come back with:

"So, I guess it's a choice for you to be straight then?"

And every time, I get the satisfaction of watching the stupid looks on their faces as they try to process what I have just asked them.

Midsumma was just the start of Tania's gay adventure. Having Tan in my life again was the best thing to happen. Knowing that there were now two of us in the family that was gay made me feel less of a freak. That there was nothing wrong with me. It obviously runs in the family. Well, that's how I like to think of it anyway. Having my own flesh and blood be the same as me made me feel so loved and connected which made my bond with Tania grow stronger.

We started going to a lesbian night called 'Girl Bar' in a club in St Kilda. It was that night we met Belinda. Belinda, an edgy chick of Italian heritage, a sleeve tattoo on her arm, had also had just ended a long-term relationship with a guy. Sadly, people feel that they have to conform to what society or families expect of them. I felt so happy for Tan and Belinda that they were now set free and liberated. They could love whoever the fuck they want, and there is nothing wrong with that.

That night was the funniest nights of my life. Tania had gotten on a lesbian site called 'Pink Sofa' where you could meet other lesbians. Tania had met a couple online, and we met up with them at the club. Tania and I got so wasted that I kept bumping her drinks out of her hand. Every time it happened, we would look at each other in shock, then piss ourselves laughing. That night cost me at least $100 bucks in spilt drinks!

Throughout the night, we had lost Belinda all night to a tall, good-looking girl named Cecile. Cecile, an artist, was the sweetest person I have ever met. Belinda and Cecile kept disappearing throughout the night, and we would play 'Where's Belinda and Cecile?'

When we could get a visual, there Belinda was kissing, Cecile on the dance floor. We would check every hour, and they were still in the same place. *Have they come up for air yet?* I wondered. But I was happy that she had met someone. Belinda and Cecile became a part of our friendship group, a family of gays and lesbians that we nicknamed our 'gaymily.'

I am such a lucky guy to have such a great group of wonderful humans in my life. My friendship with Belinda and Cecile is coming around to its tenth year! There have been many parties, chilled get-togethers over the years, rejuvenating off each other's loving and positive energies. When I need a recharge, I would always get together with Tania, Belinda and Cecile.

September 2010 was a particularly special year. Gay marriage was not legal in Australia, but the fight for equality was still active in the LGBTIQA+ community. Belinda and Cecile decided that they would solidify their relationship with a commitment ceremony, which we all called a wedding anyway. I was so touched to be asked to be a part of the celebration. We all gathered down the beach and with Cecile and Belinda standing in the middle of the circle, one by one, we walked up to them, placing a different coloured small rope around their wrists. The ropes symbolise lifetime unity or the everlasting union of two people, as well as a symbol of marital protection; while the loops formed signifies their love for one another.

I was so proud and honoured to be a part of something so beautiful. My favourite lesbians making their love official. I could only hope that one day, I would find my husband to share my life with.

# CHAPTER 32

# LAST TEN YEARS

It was August 2012, and I was still in recovery from my ice-skating accident. I hadn't skated since I was five years old when I was living with my Nan and Pop. Three years ago, I had the urge to start skating again, I think I was reliving my childhood dream at thirty-three, but I loved it! I started doing the group adult skate classes starting at the beginners level.

I trained at the Olympic skating rink in Docklands, Melbourne, and this place was huge! It had two full skating rinks, one was mainly for the group lessons, and ice hockey training and club games and the other was for general skating and the figure skating coaching sessions, and this was my goal.

In the beginning, I had moved through the skating group lessons quickly, it was like riding a bike, and the coach recognised that I had started skating from a young age, as it didn't take me long to, what they call it, get my skating legs back. In the last three years, I had my own coach, was a member of the mixed adult synchronised skating team, had skated as a chorus member in the 2010 Christmas Ice Show.

In 2010, I was also in my first year of my second bachelor's degree studying a Bachelor of Health Science in Myotherapy. Myotherapy is an evidence-based form of physical therapy which focuses on the assessment, treatment and rehabilitation of musculoskeletal pain and associated conditions.

When I had completed my three-year degree in Myotherapy in 2012, I worked as a sub-contractor for a multidisciplinary chiropractic clinic thirty minutes from my studio apartment in

St Kilda West. The owners of the clinic, Cara and Nick were the nicest, caring people I had met. Cara had been working as a chiropractor for the past twenty years, and James was an acupuncturist. They had been married for the past 16 years and lived only ten minutes from the clinic.

I had taken six months off skating so I could concentrate on finishing my degree and skating was expensive, and being a student, I found it challenging to find the money for rink hire and to pay for my lessons. It was June 2012, when I started working full time, and now the money was not an issue, I could afford to resume skating again. I was so excited to be back on the ice still.

Miranda, a junior chiropractor, jokingly said that I'm going to have so many injuries. Well, I think she jinxes me because on my first morning back at training I had my accident that would end my skating forever. The thing I loved most about skating was the feeling of being free.

Gliding around the rink with the cool breeze on your face and the juxtaposition between the strength in your leg and core muscles used for speed, catapulting from the ice into the air and landing your jumps on a thin blade while being elegant and graceful at the same time. I was ready to start training and enter this season adult skating competitions.

Being my first training session back, I should have just kept to the basic warmups, working the edges of my skates, getting a feel for the ice again, getting my skate legs back. But I got too confident and tried a basic jump that I had done a hundred times before *the single Salchow.*

*The single Salchow jump is commonly done from a forward outside three turn. After the three turns, the skater stops momentarily with the free foot extended behind, then swings the free leg forward and around with a wide scooping motion, jumping in the air and landing back on the former free foot.*

The reason I should not have been jumping is that I had my blades sharpened the day before, and you're supposed to wear them in first. As I was landing the single Salchow, which is only half a full turn, my landing blade got stuck in the ice, and my body kept turning, and before I hit the ground, I heard a defining *POP, CRACK!*

Now, when you fall your instincts is to get back up again. But, as I tried to stand back up my coach screamed, "DON'T GET UP! DON'T GET UP!" As I looked down towards the bottom of my right leg, I could see my heel facing me. I had dislocated my ankle and broke my fibula (the bone on the outside of your leg). "FUCK!" I yelled as I sat back down on the ice. As soon as I saw my ankle, then the pain came rushing in, and all I could do was lay on the Ice.

They administered first aid, laying me on the spinal board to get me off the cold ice and called an ambulance. The pain was so intense, and I thought I need to distract myself. As I lay there watching the other skaters train, some coming up to see if I was ok, then seeing their faces turn white when they saw the state of my leg *that's when I felt like roadkill!*

It was only 6:30 in the morning, what was taking the ambulance so long? I thought as I tried to breathe through the pain of my ankle swelling inside my tight skate. The ambulance finally arrived and immediately gave me the special green whistle of morphine. One of the ambulance officers said, "I'll have to cut this skate off". I immediately protested, "No, don't these cost me fifteen hundred dollars!". The ambulance told me that I may need another whistle and to suck on it ten times. I did as he instructed, while he carefully unlaced my skate and slowly took my foot out of it. I was so high by then I couldn't feel a thing.

The ambulance officers tied straps onto the head of the spinal board I was laying on, and pulled me off the Ice, like roadkill! I was lifted onto the stretcher and put into the back of the ambulance for my ride to the Alfred hospital in Prahran.

I must have had Tom listed as my emergency contact as he was waiting at the emergency bay. One of my coaches must have called him during the commotion. Usually, Tom has a weak stomach for this kind of thing, and I was impressed that he handled looking at my mangled ankle. Alfred being a teaching hospital, had everyone from nursing, medical and physiotherapy students gathered around to see, what I now understand having been a nursing student myself, this was a remarkable trauma to see.

The doctor advised me of my injuries and said that he will have to sedate me using Ketamine to be able to relocate my ankle and plaster my leg, ready for surgery. Now, ironically, I used to use Ketamine (K, Ket, Special K) as a party drug or to get high and have threesomes with sexy guys.

Already high off the green whistles I smiled and said,

"Oh, I haven't had K in years!" I said groggily.

Tom started laughing, but unfortunately, the Doctor didn't see my humour. When I woke up, my right leg was in plaster from my foot up past my knee. Tom was sitting beside me,

"How are you going potty mouth?" he laughed

"What" I said, confused.

"When the doctor came back to tell you what they had done, you were like, oh fuck! Really! Fuck" he said.

"Oh, no way!" I started laughing.

Tom had called my work, Dan, Ally, and Tom's sisters Kate and Lucy to know what has happened. At midnight I was taken into surgery and had the break in my fibula screwed together and a new smaller cast put on my leg. Lucy came into the hospital the next day with snacks and my laptop to keep me occupied.

I was lucky Lucy was on her holidays from work. For the next eight weeks, I was in recovery. I was sent home with strong pain killers, and it didn't take long to get addicted to them. When one of the nurses at the hospital asked me if I had a drug problem in the past, I lied and said no in the fear I wouldn't get good enough pain killers as I have a low tolerance to pain.

Before my accident I had agreed to house sit Tom and Isabelle's place in Thornbury, north side of the city, to feed Tom's cat Tiah, while they travelled to New York for a four-week holiday. My studio apartment in St Kilda had three flights of stairs outside that would have made it too dangerous for me to navigate, so I lived for a month in Thornbury.

A couple of years ago, sadly, Tom and Marie divorced. It's not my place to discuss the reasons why their marriage broke down in a forum such as this book. All I can say is that Tom is now happily married with his 2nd wife Isabelle and they have a beautiful son, my nephew, we all call 'Little Man'. Isabelle is a tall, beautiful looking women with long dark hair. She is a great wife, mother and has become a great friend and sister in law to me.

I had a lot of time to myself, and I don't like living in my head as the negative thoughts become too loud. I would start taking more of the painkillers to knock me out so I could sleep the days away. People would visit, but that was mostly on weekends, so during the weekdays, I was alone.

I became depressed again, feeling hopeless and sorry for myself. Getting into the shower was a difficult task in itself, leaving me feeling exhausted, so I would shower every three days. I was so happy to get the cast off and into the moon boot so I could at least walk around again. I could see that I was relying on the painkillers, not for physical pain relief, but to numb the mental pain I was feeling. Before Tom and Isabelle came back to New York, I stopped taking the pills and went cold turkey.

I could ease the pain with paracetamol, so there was no need for the painkillers anymore. Cara and Nick were so generous, that they offered to have me stay with them so I could go back to work and do admin work until I could go back to massaging again. It was a long recovery, but with the help of some special people in my life, I got through it. After some physical therapy, I was on my feet again, but I was too scared to go back to skating. I thought about it, but after weighing up what I have been through, I decided to hang my skates up for good.

With my addictive personality, I knew I was skating on thin ice, and if I had kept on self-medicating myself, I could have turned a darker path of becoming a full-blown prescription medication addict. After two and a half months, I was back in my St Kilda West studio apartment, and my life was getting back to normal again. Friday after work, I would come home to an empty apartment, and this is when I would feel the most depressed, *I was lonely.*

I tried to fill that void by hooking up with different guys off Grinder, the gay dating app, but these guys were just a band-aid. Getting sick of guys just wanting sex and frustrated that no one wanted to go on dates, I realised that maybe I'm using the wrong platform. So, I looked at dating websites, and I thought that perhaps there are guys on here that are after something a bit more substantial? And that's when I met Brendan Prosser.

# CHAPTER 33

# BRENDAN

I wish this were my happy ever after story, that I could say that all my dreams were realised – but I can't. What I can say is that I finally learnt and felt what it was like to be loved by someone unconditionally. All the red flags were there, but I chose to ignore them. I had met Brendan via an online dating site. We messaged back and forth for a few weeks. Brendan said he had his mother's wedding coming up and that this was her third husband. But the man she was marrying was a good man and treated her well, and that was all that mattered.

He took a selfie of himself in his black shirt that he was wearing to the wedding. He looks handsome, I thought. A few more weeks went by, and I didn't hear from him, so I thought, oh well, that was short lived. I didn't expect to hear any more from him, this is the general pattern in the gay world, not many guys wanting something meaningful- just a quick shag. So, I didn't think any more of it.

The next day I logged into my account on the dating site. To my surprise, there was a message from Brendan.

*Hi there! Sorry for the late reply. It's been a busy week. Would still like to meet you though.*

We organised to meet, and he was going to come over to my place on Friday night. I was excited and nervous at the same time; it had been a long time since I went on a proper date. When I felt like male company, I would go onto Grindr or Scruff, the gay apps, and find a guy to come over for sex. Tom would joke saying that it was like ordering pizza, see what you like and order it. But I was getting sick of the meaningless connections and although fun and exhilarating at the time, afterwards, I just felt lonelier than before. I was thirty-four years old, and I was ready for something more.

Brendan and I were together for three and a half years before we separated. Together we had made a home in a new apartment complex in Hampton. We moved in together after only seeing each other for four weeks in August 2013. I have a fixer, saviour personality, and I thought that I would be able to save Brendan and find love at the same time.

During that initial four weeks of dating, Brendan was admitted into a private psychiatric facility for his depression, anxiety and personality disorder alongside his alcohol issues. He told me that he had been struggling with alcohol abuse for many years. That should have been enough for me to run, but Brendan looked like a broken man in need of someone to be his support. He was so vulnerable, and his big brown eyes and his charm melted my heart, and I fell in love with him. It was funny because our 2nd date was taking him to see a movie on his approved leave from the hospital. But I didn't care about that. I didn't see someone with mental health or a prescription drug and alcohol problem, all I saw was a guy that needed someone.

I do admit that I wanted to fix, to save him, and I honestly thought that I could help him get through this bad patch and we could have a happy ever after story. Everyone deserves to be loved. Brendan was handsome, caring, attentive, loving, articulate, thoughtful, and talented in interior design. This was when he wasn't drunk or unwell. When the bottle was talking, and Brendan felt attacked he would know how to hit you where it really hurt, he had a talent for spReying vile words that could cut you deep.

If he couldn't get to you face to face, he would via text message or emails, which in this case his poor family would cop, especially his mother, Jill. The worst thing Brendan said to me during an argument while he was full of wine was "No wonder why your parents didn't want you!" I couldn't believe he would use my past trauma against me. When he sobered up, he was remorseful, and even though I could forgive him for it, once you hear something, you can never un-hear it. I think this was the moment I started to fall out of love with him. But I still loved him, I just wasn't in love with him, and we were at the two-year mark in our relationship.

Going back to our first year together, it was the year 2013 when Brendan was discharged from the hospital, he moved into my studio apartment in St Kilda West. I was running my own business as a Myotherapist and Personal trainer out of a gym. Brendan used to work as a property manager in rental real estate. His mother Jill and her second husband had started their own real estate business when Brendan was eighteen, and that is how Brendan began in the real estate industry. Jill would tell me how good he was at the job.

During this time his family had money and Brendan, of course, liked the luxury cars and houses. Brendan had found a new one-bedroom apartment located 10 minutes walk from the beach in Hampton. I thought my dreams had come true. I found a partner that I could start a life with, and I had always dreamed of setting up a home with. This made me full whole, loved and content.

Brendan had a large family. During Jill's second marriage to Peter, they had two children together Eliza and George, who are one year apart in age. Peter had a son, Duncan, who was around Brendan's sisters Sarah age, Brendan being the oldest. It's not my place to discuss in this book what had happened to end Jill's marriage to Peter. But from Brendan's experience growing up as a teenager, he had a complicated relationship with his step farther. When Brendan was in his late teens, he started experimenting with drugs and alcohol.

Graham, Jill's third husband, had two sons from his previous marriage, Jorden and Nathan, who were young adults when I met them. Brendan's family were like the real-life 'Brady Bunch', and I loved them all. Whenever I met a partner, I always wanted to be accepted into their family. I thought I was so lucky to have this, and I would get so mad at Brendan, how he would take it for granted and often get the family offside. I couldn't understand how he couldn't see the support he could have if he embraced his family instead of pushing them away.

During our first year together, I tried to get him to see a psychologist to get psychotherapy, but when the trauma would resurface Brendan would stop attending his sessions. I encouraged him to keep going and face his trauma like I had done with therapy, as the outcomes have rewards, and you can move on with your life. Unfortunately, Brendan's resolution to his childhood trauma was the bottle and his benzodiazepine prescription drugs.

I loved Brendan's family. His family home in Warrandyte, a suburb located in the north-east area 24 kilometres from Melbourne's central business district. They were so welcoming, and it wasn't long before I became a part of the family. When

Brendan and I had a fight, and he would start his rants, or when he would start on Jill, Jill was my ally, and I was hers. We would call each other and begin with, "Now don't tell Brendan, but…" We were each other's support, which brought close and bonded our relationship as her son-in-law.

It was the day before Christmas Eve 2013, and I asked Brendan if we could add an addition to our family, a kitten. Brendan was keen on the Idea, and I looked on a site called Gumtree, which is an online community classifieds platform. This is where we found our fur baby. We named him Jackson. He was advertised as free to a good home, the runt of the litter. So, the next morning, we drove to the western suburbs to collect our son.

Jackson, a black and white kitten with mainly white on his tummy, grew into a mischievous, will of his own, playful but naughty personality. Like Brendan. When Jackson was six months old, I thought it would be best if he had a playmate. The RSPCA advertised free adoption of kittens and cats during their winter appeal.

Brendan and I went to the RSPCA pound and found a little, timid, abandoned, six-month-old tabby female kitten. Once she came to trust you, she would show you love and affection. Like me. There we had a small family. It was funny because Jackson, who was like Brendan's personality, became my cat and Baily who was like my personality, became Brendan's cat. We both became their daddies.

During this time Brendan really tried to stay sober. Jill and Graham would drive out every Sunday morning to Hampton from Warrandyte to take Brendan to Alcoholics Anonymous.

As a family, we would support Brendan, but this only lasted around two months before Brendan stopped going, saying the people there gave him anxiety when they all pounce on him to talk after the meetings.

Brendan said he could do it on his own, with my help, but it wasn't long before he relapsed and started drinking again. Then he would promise to get sober, and things would be great until the cycle began again. Having my own issues with mental illness and past drug addiction, I think, made me more tolerant and patient because I understood the difficulties.

When things were good, they were really good, and when they were bad, they were really bad. During the good times, we would spend winter weekends enjoying a Sunday drive to the Peninsula Hot Springs, enjoying the relaxing thermal pools. On the way home, we would walk along the beach and get fish 'n' chips for a late lunch.

We were like best friends in a co-dependent relationship. Other times we would drive up to a small town called Sassafras located in the Dandenong's, famous for their Devonshire tea and large scones with strawberry jam and cream.

I look back on time we spent together, these are the memories I hold dear. I just wish he could have overcome his demons and get real help, worked on his sobriety and stuck at therapy for his past traumas. If he did, I believe we could have made a real go of things and had a happy life together, even gotten married.

I loved spending time with his family, especially Christmas. Brendan and I would drive up to Torquay on Christmas Eve and stay at Kate and Toby's house with Lilly. Tom and Alice would drive up Christmas morning to have Christmas lunch together, then Brendan and I would drive to his parents in Warrandyte. Christmas Eve 2014 was a significant year for Brendan as at midnight mass at a small Anglican church in Torquay, Brendan was touched by God. During the service before communion, people were invited up the front to receive a blessing by the pastor.

To our surprise, Brendan went up to the front. It was a beautiful moment, and Brendan seemed really at peace. He never said what he was thinking or what he said to God, and I never asked as this was between Brendan and the big guy upstairs. But I had never seen Brendan so calm and peaceful. I wish this were enough to have set Brendan on a path of healing, but unfortunately, it wasn't enough. Every Christmas, Brendan was the happiest to both our families.

When we arrived at Brendan's family home for Christmas dinner, I received an extraordinary gift. We were sitting in the lounge handing out presents and Eliza, and Jill handed me a small wrapped box first. On the Christmas tree were coloured ball ornaments with all the kid's names written on them. When I opened my carefully wrapped box, inside was my own ball ornament with *Shane* written on it in silver glitter. Jill said that I was now officially apart of their family, and this was so special to me.

The year 2015 would be a significant year for Brendan and I. Brendan had started a job debt collecting for a major electricity company, and I was beginning my 1st year at Victoria University undertaking a Bachelor of Nursing Degree. This was my third degree, but who's counting. I was becoming exhausted working in my business and decided to close it down and go back to my old massage job at the chiropractor's clinic casually while completing my nursing degree.

Brendan was very supportive and became the breadwinner of the family. I'm not sure if it was the stress of working full-time, but Brendan would bring home 2-3 bottles of wine home every Friday night and drink until he passed out on the couch. If I protested about his drinking, he would turn on me and, in the end, I just stopped saying anything and kept out of his way. Hard to do when you live in a one-bedroom apartment.

Every Friday afternoon I would get anxious because I knew that Brendan would drink, and I didn't know which Brendan I would be coming home too. Every Friday night, we would have dinner, and he would start drinking. I would go into our room close the sliding door that separated our bedroom from the lounge room and hide with the cats, while I watched TV shows I would download the day before.

Brendan would watch his TV shows in the lounge room and drink until he passed out. Brendan would question why I just spend time in the bedroom and not with him, and I would tell him I was just exhausted from work and uni. I tried to downplay it as to not set him off. My mental health became affected, and I had put on a lot of weight from stress.

In the end, I just couldn't do it anymore. Brendan had no intention of changing, and his drinking became a significant problem in our relationship. September 2016, I left him. This was the hardest thing I did as I was afraid that he would harm himself or suicide, as he often would threaten to do if I ever left him. Even though we had loved each other and depended on each other, I had to break this toxic cycle as it wasn't doing either of us any good.

I guess, when two broken people with a traumatic childhood try and develop a meaningful relationship, when they haven't really recovered from their past, they're bound to make a mess of the relationship. That is what Brendan and I did. Our relationship became a toxic and dependent relationship in which the cycle needed to be broken. After loving someone for three and a half years, it took a lot of courage to leave, and as painful and scary as it was to go it alone again, I finally broke the cycle.

# CHAPTER 34

# GONE FOREVER

It was Wednesday night, 7<sup>th</sup> March 2018, when I got the call from Jill to tell me Bren was no longer with us, that he had passed.

*No! No! No!*

"How?" I asked her.

There was silence. I could tell Jill was struggling to get the words out, but she didn't have to say it because, in the pit of my stomach, I already knew the answer.

"He hung himself love" she replied, holding back her tears.

"When?" I asked.

"He was found this afternoon by the next-door neighbour. He could smell a strong odour coming from Bren's apartment. He jumped over the balcony divider on Bren's, and the glass sliding door was open, Bren must have left it open enough for the cats to go in and out. Once the neighbour walked inside, he could see Bren's body slumped over down the hallway. He suddenly left the apartment and called the police" Jill informed me.

"I have to go now, let's talk tomorrow" Jill hung up.

She sounded like she was in shock, like me. I couldn't believe this has happened. I only spoke to him last week via messenger. When we separated, this was my biggest fear, that one day I would get the call. Tonight, was that night. I was in shock, my throat tightened, and as I climbed off my bed, my legs gave way, and I fell onto the floor. As I stared blankly at the door, my tears started rolling down my face as I tried to make sense of the news. I stood up and walked across the hall to Ally's bedroom and knocked on her door.

"Yeah" Ally called out,

As I walked into her bedroom, she was shocked at my state.

"What"s wrong?' she asked.

"Bren hung himself in the apartment. His body was discovered today."

"Oh, Shit! I'm so sorry, Shane."

As I climbed onto her bed, Jake came up from his sleeping spot and licked my face, concerned that I was upset. Like a child, I curled up into a ball and lay my head on Ally's lap. Then it happened, my scream of anguish echoed through the room, and I lay there sobbing while Ally tried to comfort me. Jake, being the beautiful boy, laid next to me, placing his head near my face and his paw in my hand. Ally had adopted Jake around four months before I moved in. Jake, a mixed breed of Staffie and Labrador aged around nine years old. Became my life saver. Ally did shift work, and I would help walk and feed Jake, so in a way, he became my best mate.

Brendan and I had been separated for sixteen months. I had moved in with Ally in her two-bedroom apartment in Bentleigh East end of September 2017. I was halfway through the 2nd year of my nursing degree when I left Brendan. It was the hardest thing I ever had to do. I only wish he could have tried harder to stop drinking and get off his benzodiazepines, then maybe we could have had a happy life together. I know how hard it must have been for him, but I wish he had tried harder. When I left midway through September 2016, I lived with Kate, her husband Mike and their daughter Darsh for a year in the surf coast town Torquay. Lucky, I had met Tom back in 1997 and became a part of his family because they were always there for me. Without Lilly, Kate or Mike I would have been homeless when I left Brendan.

I was lucky to have met Christie at uni. Christie was forty-six years old Italian women who were married with three children, two girls and one boy. Sally, aged 17, Molly 20 and Rick 14 years old. Her husband's name was Cam. During the final year of our degree, Christie and I chose the same classes so I could stay with them, so I didn't have to travel back and forth from Torquay to St Albans, where our Victoria University campus was located. I was so grateful the Christie and her family. I wouldn't have been able to complete my degree without them.

You know you have real loyal friends, the ones that are your family, and that is who Ally, Dan and Monte were to me. No matter what happened in our lives or how busy I had gotten trying to juggle a relationship, full-time study and part-time work; Ally, Dan and Monte were always around when I needed them. Through Ally, we had met a couple of new additions to our family, Tan and Mich. When I had moved in with Ally, our group enjoyed dinners Ally would cook together, go on a couple of weekend trips to Sydney and I was so happy to have reconnected with them again.

After I got myself together, Ally told me to have one of my Valium tablets to help calm me. "Thanks, Ally," I said as I got off the bed.

"Are you going to be OK?" she asked.

"Yeah I'll be fine, I'll call Tom" I said as I closed the door behind me.

I took a Valium and called Tom. "Hey Shane" he answered.

I couldn't speak and started crying. "What's happened?" he asked.

"Bren hung himself, he's dead" answering once I could get the words out.

"Oh, fuck! Shit! No!"

He sounded shocked like the rest of us. He told me that he was coming over. I told him he didn't have to that I would be fine, but he insisted. Tom drove the forty-minute drive from his place to mine, and by the time he got there, it was nearly midnight. I was touched that he went out of his way to be there for me – his brother.

I filled him in with what Jill had told me. We talked. He hugged me while I cried. I looked through my messages on my phone from when I last heard from Brendan, it had been about a week from his last message till the time his body was found.

When I realised that he could have been dead for four to five days before his neighbour found him, I felt so guilty – *I could have done something! I could have saved him!* Tom reassured me that it wasn't my fault, that we were separated and that it was Brendan's choice to end his life. Tom stayed for about an hour, I felt bad as it was so late, I could see the worry he had on his face.

"You're not going to do anything stupid are you?" he asked.

"No – no, I'm not" I tried to be convincing, but he didn't buy it.

"You have Ally here and if you need me just call OK?" he instructed.

"Yeah I know" I replied.

Tom left, and I went to bed. I took another Valium and cried until the effects of the pill took over and sent me to sleep.

The next day I woke up hoping the night before was a bad dream – but it wasn't. I was into the first week of my Graduate Nursing Orientation program, and today, I had to call in and explained what had happened and that I wouldn't be in today.

My graduate co-ordinator was understanding and was so supportive through my grief. I knew that Brendan wouldn't want this to affect my work as I had worked so hard to get here – I needed help because I wanted to kill myself.

Laura called me that morning. Tom must have messaged her to let her know what had happened. I told Laura that I need to go to the hospital, that I wasn't feeling safe. Ally had gone to work, and I was home alone with Jake. Lilly took me to the emergency department, and I spoke with a mental health nurse who referred me to the local community mental health service for treatment and grief counselling. I didn't want to be admitted into the inpatient ward as I had just started my Graduate Nursing Year. I was given an appointment that afternoon to see a Psychiatrist and Psychologist.

While I was at the Hospital, Jill messaged me to see if I could help collect our cats Jackson and Baily. I had left the cats with him and visited them when I would see him when I had time. I told her that I was in the hospital but could help over the weekend. I couldn't have them where I was staying because of Jake, as much as I wanted to have them, it wasn't possible, so I knew I would have to take them to a shelter to be rehomed. What I didn't know was that Brendan's father had come down from Queensland and decided to empty the apartment straight away.

Jill said that she was just in shock that she just went along with his orders, and like little worker bees, they just cleaned out his apartment. *Our apartment.* I know that Brendan and I had been separated for eighteen months, but we were best friends and I know he would've wanted me there. Jill and Sarah were kind and kept some things of Brendan's for me to keep;

the studio lamp we had brought together at Ikea, some artwork and knick-knacks. It was just a communication breakdown; everyone was in a grief-stricken state. I just wish I had been there.

We couldn't have Brendan's funeral until the coroner released his body after the autopsy was performed and the detectives completed their enquiry. Jill was sweet to have me involved in the arrangements by letting me know what was happening and asked me if I wanted to put some photos of Bren and me in the slide show. Sarah said that they had a lot of pictures of Bren in his younger years, but not many as an adult.

I picked a few photos I had of us on Facebook. The selfie he took of us together driving to the Mornington Peninsula Springs, our Sunday day trips to Sassafras in the Dandenong's. A couple of weeks went by, and Brendan's body was released. Jill invited me to meet at their house to travel with the family. I was so touched that they still considered me a part of their family.

"You kept Bren alive, and with us, for those years you were together" Jill said as she hugged me. We left the house and was driven to the funeral. It was kept small, just family and close family friends. I greeted the extended family members outside and hugged Sarah as she arrived with her husband, Jimmy. I stuck close to Duncan, George, Eliza and Nathan as we walked into the room.

As I walked into the room, the first thing I spotted was Brendan's brown mahogany coffin with brass handles on the sides, and the biggest bouquet of white lilies on the top I have ever seen. Nothing but the best for him. Brendan always enjoyed the finer things in life, I guess that's how he was brought up, those many years ago. *Brendan Andrew Prosser-18th March 1982 to 7th March 2018* was on the large projector screen with his picture.

The handsome man with brown spiky, messy hair and those big brown eyes that showed a kind, loving, sensitive, sentimental guy and that if you looked deep enough, showed his loneliness and demons that took him from us so suddenly.

I didn't have much to do with the organisation of his funeral, and I felt like a widower, even though we had been separated for sixteen months. Jill said that it was a testament to me, that Brendan would call me his best friend after we separated. Brendan had never kept in contact with any of his past ex-boyfriends.

Grief-stricken, I found comfort in this, even though our relationship was one of dependency, and toxic at times, I knew deep down Brendan loved me, and I loved him. Now in death, the loss of my best friend, my first real relationship and unconditional love is one I will grieve for a long time.

The Civil Celebrant did an excellent introduction to Brendan's service and highlighted his cheekiness and humour.

"When Brendan was 8 years old, he came home from school one day and asked his grandmother what a lesbian was."

Everyone in the room chuckled as we all knew Brendan's mischievous humour. When he was sober and mentally well, he was a beautiful, loving soul who cared deeply for his family and was a loyal partner to me, and that's the Brendan I wanted to remember.

There were fun times in our relationship, like the night we went through Mc Donald's drive-through for dinner on Sunday night, and Brendan tricked me into ordering a 'McClucky meal' instead of an Mc Chicken meal. The poor teenage girl serving us seemed so confused, and when I realised what I had ordered, Brendan was already laughing in the passenger seat.

I was first up to give my eulogy. I was nervous, I didn't know how I would get through it without howling halfway through. Jill came up and stood beside me and held my hand.


*Dear Brendan,*

*I just wanted to thank you for loving me unconditionally. You were a caring, sensitive, loving and loyal guy. I will cherish the great times we had together over our three and a half years we had together. When we first decided to move in together, Brendan used his real estate expertise and found a brand-new apartment to rent in Hampton.*

*Christmas 2014, we adopted our fur babies Jackson and Baily, and we had our own little family. Brendan loved decorating the apartment and each week would come home with some new knick-knack or art piece, and our apartment started to look like a homewares store.*

*Brendan loved our Sunday day trips to Sassafras in the Dandenong's where we would have scones and hot chocolate, our walks along Hampton Beach. He was very much loved by my family, his charm won everyone over.*

*Brendan gave me a special gift and that was meeting the Prosser / Mitchener and Mcintyre family. I had a great mother and father-in-law Jill and Graham, new brothers Duncan, George, Nathan and Jorden and sisters Sarah and Eliza that I could call family. Brendan loved you all very much.*

*When Brendan and I separated, we remained best friends. He was my soul mate, and I will always love him dearly. Brendan's last words to me were "Concentrate on your nursing, and help others like you have helped me", and that's what I will do in honour of Brendan's memory.*

*Through the pain of losing my best friend, I take comfort in that God has you now, and you are at peace. I will never forget you and like what we would always say to each other "I Love You to the Moon and Back".*

I made it through the eulogy with only a couple of times to stop and compose myself. I took my seat next to Eliza, and Jill spoke about Brendan's younger years, how he was a cheeky kid with a great sense of humour that would push the boundaries, how it gave him great enjoyment to see peoples shocked reactions. Brendan was Jill's first born and as his mother, never turned her back on him even when he was horrible to her. Sitting behind me, George broke down. I could feel his pain; he had lost his big brother. Brendan alienated his siblings with his behaviour, and they hadn't spoken to him for months. Even though Brendan acted like he didn't care, I know that this would have caused him great pain but was just too proud to show it.

At the end of the service, Bren's casket was wheeled past us down the aisle as we all followed him out. We all watched him being placed in the back of the black hearse. I hugged George as we watched the hearse drive down the road and into the distance of the cemetery. Tears streamed down my face as I watch the man I once loved, sometimes my enemy, always my best friend, fade into the distance until the hearse was no longer to be seen – Brendan was gone.

Brendan Andrew Prosser

18/03/1982 to 07/03/2018

# EPILOGUE

I have good and bad days. In public, at work around friends, I'm the bubbly, funny Shane. In private and left to my own thoughts, I'm depressed. I try to push through because that's what I have always done. It's been ingrained in me from the age of 5 years old. Survival.

I try to keep busy. Full-time Nursing Career. Post Graduate Study. Varied extracurricular activities, all to get me out of my head. Too long alone left with my thoughts could be dangerous. The circle of grief jumps from denial and disbelief that Brendan is gone, to anger and resentment that he didn't fight harder, and my own guilt – I should have saved him.

With Brendan, I thought I had built my own little family. We raised a little fur babies Jackson and Bailey; we created a home in our one-bedroom apartment in the coastal suburb of Hampton near the bay. But that's all gone now.

Losing him to suicide sent me to the psychiatric hospital as I wanted to kill myself. Instead of being admitted into the hospital, I began treatment for my depression through the southeast mental health community clinic as an outpatient. I had worked too hard during my three-year nursing degree and endured nerve-racking interviews to secure employment in a Mental Health Nursing Graduate Program to give it all up now. I know Brendan wouldn't want that.

"Just concentrate on your nursing" was Brendan's final text message to me. A year later, I still haven't been able to delete our last conversation via text from my phone. With time it gets easier. The sun is starting to shine through the cracks of those stormy clouds.

I feel all my life; I have fought continuously for survival. Sometimes I feel like I'm sick of fighting. Sleep. Never wake up. Peace. Then I have to remind myself of all that I have achieved and overcome in my life. The close friendships I have made. My *Familia*. My protective factors. I couldn't leave them hurting by ending my life.

Now, I try and stay on the positive side of life. Helping others give me purpose and make me feel like I'm giving back in some small way. As a Mental Health Nurse with lived experience, I think it gives you some street cred with the consumers as I truly understand what some of them are going through. Because I have lived through my own trauma, mental health issues and drug addiction. Exercise helps keep me well as medications can only do so much. But I'm only human and can get lazy in that department sometimes. I just take each day as it comes.

So, I'll just keep on fighting. My mental health issues won't defeat me. I have a lot to live for!

I am resilient!

My Foster Mum Joan Graham and I at my
Bachelor of Nursing Graduation May 2019

# ACKNOWLEDGEMENTS

When I set the ambitious task of writing my memoir, I hadn't fully appreciated what was really involved. That last six months of writing has been a roller coaster of emotions as I read through my foster care file. Having seen what the social workers, my foster parents and my biological family have said about you in black and white, was like exposure therapy. But, through this process, I had an incredible support network.

So, I would like to thank my friends and family for their ongoing support during this journey. John Burgess for his assistance with Marketing through his Marketing & Communications creative agency 'Little Rocket' and being my support and friend for the last 21 years. Belinda Raposo, my talented senior editor for this book, your friendship and encouragement throughout this writing process, is what has kept me on track.

Dave and his team at Green Hill Publishing for all your hard work in making my dream become a reality. Wendy from WMC Public Relations for believing in my book and supporting me through the promotion and getting my story out there. Lisa and the team at OZ Child, my foster care agency when I was in care, for all your support and generous sponsorship, which enabled me to reach my financial target to get this book produced.

Lastly, I would like to extend my thanks and gratitude to all my friends, family and supporters for not only purchasing my book but also cheering me on through my marathon journey as I tackled writing my first memoir novel. If my story can help at least one person, then that would be the icing on the cake.

# BECOMING A FOSTER CARER

Becoming a foster carer is a way of giving back to your community. There are different types of fostering available, and anyone can become a carer; Singles, Married and Defacto Couples, Same Sex Attracted Couples & Singles and retirees.

Want to know more about how to become a Foster Carer? Then please contact representatives in your state.

*Victoria*

**Fostering Connections** Call 1800 013 088 or visit the website www.fosteringconnections.com.au

**Interstate Key assets** – *The Children Services Provider* Call 1800 We Care or visit website www.canifoster.com.au

# WHERE TO FIND SUPPORT

**For Emergencies call 000**

**Beyond Blue**

*Beyond Blue* provides information and support to help everyone in Australia achieve their best possible mental health, whatever their age and wherever they live.

Call 1300 224 636 | www.beyondblue.org.au

**Lifeline**

Is a national charity providing all Australians experiencing a personal crisis with access to 24-hour crisis support and suicide prevention services.

Call 13 11 14 | www.lifeline.org.au

**Kids Help Line**

We are Kids Helpline. Kids Helpline is Australia's only free, private and confidential 24/7 phone and online counselling service for young people aged 5 to 25.

Call 1800 55 1800 | www.kidshelpline.com.au

**SANE Australia**

SANE Australia is a national mental health charity working to provide better support and stronger connections with people affected by complex mental illness.

Call 1500 18 7263 | www.sane.org

**Black Dog Institute**

The Black Dog Institute aims to improve the lives of people affected by mental illness through the rapid translation of high-quality research into improved clinical treatments, increased accessibility to mental health services and delivery of long-term public health solutions. They also provide free online mental health programs for all Australians.

www.blackdoginstitute.org.au

**Headspace (16-25 years)**

Headspace provides youth mental health confidential services for Australians aged 12-25.

www.headspace.org.au

**Create Foundation**

CREATE Foundation - The national peak consumer body representing the voices of children and young people with an out-of-home care experience.

(03) 9918 0002 | www.create.org.au

**Thorne Harbour Health**

Thorne Harbour Health continues to lead the response by providing a range of services which include prevention education, treatment and care of PLHIV and counselling services.

www.thorneharbour.org